The Tech-Savvy Booktalker

The Tech-Savvy Booktalker

A Guide for 21st-Century Educators

Nancy J. Keane and Terence W. Cavanaugh

LIBRARIES

U N L I M I T E D

A Member of the Greenwood Publishing Group

Westport, Connecticut • London

Library of Congress Cataloging-in-Publication Data

Keane, Nancy J.
  The tech-savvy booktalker : a guide for 21st-century educators / Nancy J. Keane and Terence W. Cavanaugh.
     p. cm.
  Includes bibliographical references and index.
  ISBN 978–1–59158–637–1 (alk. paper)
  1. Book talks—Technological innovations.   2. Reading promotion—Technological innovations.   3. Media programs (Education).   4. Language arts (Middle school)—Activity programs.   5. Language arts (Secondary)—Activity programs.   6. Information technology—Study and teaching (Middle school).   7. Information technology—Study and teaching (Secondary).   I. Cavanaugh, Terence W.   II. Title.
  Z1003.15.K43   2009
  021.7—dc22   2008038988

British Library Cataloguing in Publication Data is available.

Copyright © 2009 by Libraries Unlimited

Library of Congress Catalog Card Number: 2008038988
ISBN: 978–1–59158–637–1

First published in 2009

Libraries Unlimited, 88 Post Road West, Westport, CT 06881
A Member of the Greenwood Publishing Group, Inc.
www.lu.com

Printed in the United States of America

The paper used in this book complies with the Permanent Paper Standard issued by the National Information Standards Organization (Z39.48–1984).

10 9 8 7 6 5 4 3 2 1

Copyright Acknowledgments

The authors and publisher gratefully acknowledge permission for use of the following material:
Adobe product screen shot(s) reprinted with permission from Adobe Systems Incorporated.
Microsoft product screen shot(s) reprinted with permission from Microsoft Incorporated.
Apple product screen shot(s) reprinted courtesy of Apple.
Book cover from LIFE AS WE KNEW IT, Copyright 2006 by Susan Beth Pfeffer, reprinted by permission of Houghton Mifflin Harcourt Publishing Company.
Book cover from DAIRY QUEEN: a novel by Catherine Gilbert Murdock. Copyright 2006 by Catherine Gilbert Murdock. Reprinted by permission of Houghton Mifflin Harcourt Publishing Company. All rights reserved.
Book cover from RULES by Cynthia Lord. Copyright 2006 by Cynthia Lord. Reprinted by permission of Scholastic. Rubber duck detail © Gary Doak/Photonica. Goldfish detail © G.K. & Vikki Hart/Iconica.
The term "Digital Booktalk" was originally coined in 2002 by Robert Kenny, a professor at the University of Central Florida, and is a registered trademark. Parts of the curriculum found in chapters 2 and 8 are based on copyrighted materials owned by Glenda Gunter and Robert Kenny and any appearance in this book is provided under their limited permission: no photocopy or other rights to repurposing this material is provided.

To all the Ks—NJK

For James, the real writer of the family—TWC

Acknowledgments

Thanks, Cathy, for the editing.

Contents

Introduction

Talking about books and using booktalks have been tools that teachers and library media specialists effectively use as part of the reading program and to encourage reading. Integrating technology with booktalks and student participation can promote reading, writing, and speaking skills. Research has found booktalks to be a successful tool to help guide students' reading, and they can now be expanded to be multimedia activities. The 2000 National Reading Panel Report on the motivational effect of computers stated that the "rapid development of capabilities of computer technology, particularly in speech recognition and multimedia presentations, promises even more successful applications in literacy for the future" (U.S. Department of Health and Human Services, 2000, pp. 6–9). Using multimedia technology tools as a strategy to create booktalks can assist students in their learning and transition to higher-level tasks.

GOALS OF THIS BOOK

The goal of this book is to provide information and instruction on how library media specialists, teachers, and students can expand and enhance the booktalk with technology.

By the time that you finish this book, you will have:

1. become aware of standards relating to the use of booktalks and technology;
2. reflected on the current impact of technology for empowering students, teachers, and library media specialists;
3. developed your own skills in using multimedia tools and considered their use with your own students;
4. developed a variety of strategies for using tools, such as the Internet, to expand or improve the educational situation.

HOW TO USE THIS BOOK

The book is divided into 11 chapters organized to lead the reader from understanding tech-savvy students and booktalk concepts to familiarity with ways to use technology to enhance booktalks, such as by using multimedia. The sequence of the chapters was selected to cover a variety of technology implementations; however, experienced computer users should feel comfortable skipping around chapters. In the book chapters focusing on types of technology enhanced booktalks, effort was made to include the various operating systems or platforms that are in use today, including: Windows, Macintosh, and Linux.

Chapter 1 introduces the concept of booktalks.

Chapter 2 focuses on booktalk technologies and educational standards.

Chapter 3 provides information and strategies for creating text-based booktalks.

Chapter 4 has information concerning the creation of images.

Chapter 5 provides instruction for creating booktalks with presentation tools.

Chapter 6 provides instructions for creating audio booktalks.

Chapter 7 explains about creating audio and effective microphone use.

Chapter 8 provides instructions for creating video booktalks, from using stills to motion sequences.

Chapter 9 explains how to create a booktalk kiosk for a library or common room.

Chapter 10 provides additional online resources for booktalks and book discussions.

Chapter 11 provides several rubrics used in assessment.

REFERENCE

U.S. Department of Health and Human Services. (2000). Chapter 6: Computer Technology and Reading. *Instruction Reports of the Subgroups Report of the National Reading Panel: Teaching Children to Read*. Retrieved September, 2004, from http://www.nichd.nih.gov/publications/nrp/report.htm.

1

Booktalking Concepts

The booktalk is "a little piece of pie so good that it tempts one to consume the whole concoction."

— Margaret Edwards

Children's and Young Adult literature has long been a fundamental part of children's lives. Stories reflect society and help children learn about their world. Children's and adolescent literature also shows students different perspectives and allows them to experience events in a nonthreatening way. Historical fiction introduces them to what life was like long ago. Literary fiction introduced them to the beauty of language. And literature can also present valuable information and ideas about mathematics, science, and so on. Fiction makes difficult concepts accessible because it is told in a way that is understandable for many. By using literature to teach young learners, the door is open to expand the exploration of topics more in depth.

Teachers, parents, and library media specialists have tried a variety of methods to entice students to read. Surrounding a child with print is by far the most important enticement for children to embrace print. This is why our homes, classrooms, and libraries should offer the child a cacophony of print of all types. Years of research support the importance of reading to success in life.

But how important is being read to or reading independently to the child's reading ability? When the **International Association for the Evaluation of Educational Achievement (IEA)** compared the reading skills of 210,000 students from 32 different countries, it found the highest scores (regardless of income level) among:

- children who were read to by their teachers;
- children who read the most pages for pleasure daily (Elley, 1992).

If children start *reading* for pleasure, good things will follow. *Reading* comprehension will improve. Their writing and vocabulary—even spelling and grammar—will get better. In other words, readers who read for pleasure are on the road to success. Those who do not develop a pleasure *reading* habit "will have a difficult time *reading* and writing at a level high enough to deal with the demands of today's world" (Krashen, 2004, p. x).

But how to we get the children to read? One way to excite students about reading is to use booktalks. Booktalks are short promotional presentations that entice the

Booktalk Basics

What exactly is a booktalk?
A booktalk is like a movie trailer. The idea is to "sell" the book. You want to give enough information to lure the audience into wanting more.

Is a booktalk like a book review?
No. A booktalk is not a review. You don't need to say whether you liked the book or not. It is assumed that it is worth reading because you are promoting it. You might say you found it amusing or entertaining, but you really don't need to say how you feel about the book.

person into wanting to know more about specific books. Books that are not promoted often stay on the shelves to collect dust. When children hear about books either through friends, the media, or though booktalks, they are more apt to take them down and read them. The first *Harry Potter* book became a success mainly because the children were talking about it. With just an initial print run of 500 copies, there was not a huge marketing campaign at first. But children telling other children and telling adults who told children, created a bestseller, so much so that the seventh book of the series, *Harry Potter and the Deathly Hallows,* sold 8.3 million copies in its first 24 hours on sale (Scholastic, 2007). There is no doubt about the power of talking about books.

Yes, students usually first browse or listen to other students when deciding what to read, and for most students, their teachers and library media specialists are further down their personal list as resources for book selection (Braeder, 1984), but booktalking can have a major effect on reading selection. In one elementary study of book circulation, researchers found that 80 percent of the students who checked out titles stated that the presented booktalks were the primary motivating reason for checking out the book and that booktalk books were selected about twice as often as other available books (Nollen, 1992). In a different study concerning adolescents, similar results were found as the booktalk titles circulation increased significantly after booktalk presentations. Interestingly, this effect occurred for an extended time, not only immediately after the booktalks (Reeder, 1991).

The purpose of this book is to introduce ways to combine students' interest in and love of technology and their need to communicate and interact with others, in this case, talk about books.

Booktalking can be a rewarding experience for both the adult and the child. Enthusiasm is infectious. The reward is connecting students to books. Booktalks are meant to be short teasers to get people interested in reading. These can be modified to reflect specific needs of the population and your own style as a booktalker. Information that should be given about the book is: author, title, publisher, and date of publication. From there on, it is up to the booktalker to decide what to talk about.

BOOKTALK PRESENTATION

Booktalks can be given by either adults or students. Booktalks can be presented in a variety of ways. The classic booktalk is given by the adult in a formal presentation to a group of students. Often several booktalks may be given that revolve around a theme. The children can listen to the booktalks and then choose their books based on their interests.

Booktalks don't always have to be presented in a formal setting. Most booktalks given in school libraries and classrooms may be more aptly called shelf-talks because they are impromptu talks about books to one or two students. This is an ideal way to target the interest of students rather than to try to find books that will appeal to a larger audience. Likewise, children booktalking to other children can bring excitement to book selection and reading.

It is hoped that teachers, parents, school library media specialists, and public librarians will find inspiration in this book to use booktalking as a starting point for the discussion of books and connecting children with books. When children begin a lesson with enthusiasm, it's sure to be a hit. (For more information on the do's and don't's of booktalks see Appendix B.)

To find out more about booktalking and to access a database of ready-to-use booktalks, visit **Booktalks—Quick and Simple** at http://www.nancykeane.com.

TYPES OF BOOKTALKS

There is no set booktalk style. These are a few of the basic types of booktalks.

Plot Driven. Give a summary of the book leaving the ending out. You may end the booktalk with a question or a challenge for the child to guess how the book ends.

Character Driven. Concentrate on a character from the book. This is usually a major character, but you can also use a minor character that the child will meet in the books. You can:

Do the booktalk from that character's perspective.
Talk about the character as if it's someone you know.
Ask the children if they would like the character as a friend.

Connections. Make comparisons to other books. The book that you use should be one that the children might have read or be familiar with.

Author Purpose. Discuss author's purpose in writing this book.

Influence. Describe an event in the author's life that influenced the writing of this book.

It's All About Me. Compare events in the book to your own life. How is it similar or different? You may also compare the events in the book to something the children are familiar with.

Scene Driven. Share a favorite event/scene from the book and tell why it is your favorite.

Criteria for Book Selection

Although booktalks can be done for any title, the booktalker will want to target those books that have a special appeal for their audience. The books chosen to booktalk are as important as the booktalks themselves. If the books being "sold" to the students have little or no appeal, the credibility of the booktalker will be compromised. You want the students to have confidence that the books you choose will be enjoyable to read.

Most booktalkers use the following criteria to select books for their repertoire.

Characters

The characters in the book are convincing and credible. The character grows throughout the story and develops in some way. The character is described so that the reader is shown both the strengths as well as the weaknesses.

Plot

The plot describes what is happening in the story. It is vital that the story has a definite beginning that sets the stage for the story and introduces the conflict. The middle of the story should show the characters' struggle to resolve the conflict. The ending of the book should show the reader a convincing resolution to the conflict and should contain an element of surprise.

Theme

The theme of the book is the main idea of the story. The theme should be basic and simple. It should reflect the developmental values inherent in growing up. It should expand the readers' vision of life in general and human nature in particular. The theme should be one of hope.

Style

How the story is told has a profound effect on the reader. The author's use of language often dictates the readers' reaction to the story. The author should employ appropriate literary devices that move the story. The tone should also be appropriate to the story being told.

Point of View

There are many ways to tell a story. It can be told in the first person. Many are told in the third person. The story depends on the point of view. The narrator should be consistent throughout the story. The narrator should only know as much as s/he could be expected to know from his/her perspective. There are books that are written from many points of view and can be quite effective, but they can also be very confusing.

Appeal

Perhaps the most important criterion for selection is audience appeal. If the story has believable characters put into a situation that children or adolescents care about, they are more apt to read the book. There are many good books published that appeal to adults but just don't appeal to children or adolescents. If we want the students to read for the sheer joy of reading and not as a school assignment, we have to offer them books that appeal to them.

HOOKS FOR BOOKS

Try some of these techniques when booktalking:

Audience Participation. Get the audience involved—they can repeat an expression from the book. Ask questions of the audience before you go into the booktalk to get them involved. This works especially well with younger students.

Shocker. Start with just a list of dry facts then jump to a shocking or exciting event.

Headlines. Refer to an article in the news and then relate it to the book you are talk-ing. You may bring in a newspaper and pretend you are reading it to show the connection.

Jump Around. Jump quickly from one scene to another—let the audience deduce the connection.

Not What It Seems. Set up one set of expectations and then pull the rug out from under the audience.

Questions. Ask a series of questions to set the mood or to pique curiosity.

Sounds and Props. Use sounds or props—clap your hands, snap your fingers, stamp your foot. Use an object to interest the audience. You can use a real object or just pantomime the object—for example, lighting a candle, playing a video game.

Themes. Talk about several books that share the same theme.

What if? Present the moral dilemma facing the central character.

It's All About You. Relate the events in the book to events in the listeners' lives.

Remember—the number one rule of booktalking is to have fun and not worry about all the other rules!

EDUCATOR COLLABORATION

Students, teachers, and library media specialists can work collaboratively in de-veloping booktalks. School librarians or media specialists can work with a teacher to identify high interest reading topics and texts and then assemble book collections or classroom book sets. The school library media specialists may present booktalks to help students in their own reading selection, but these booktalks then could also be demon-strations of effective design for booktalking development and presentation strategies.

Margaret Edwards, the mother of booktalking, stated five objectives in a book-talk:

- Sell reading for pleasure.
- Introduce new ideas and new fields of reading.
- Develop appreciation of style and character portrayal.
- Lift the level of reading by introducing the best books the audience can read with pleasure.
- Humanize books, the library, and the librarian.

WRITING THE BOOKTALK

Planning a technology enhanced booktalk begins with the basic writing of the booktalk. From there, you can decide to deliver the booktalk in a traditional face-to-face talk or in a technology-enhanced method.

The steps for writing a booktalk include:

1. Take notes as you read books for booktalks. Include: author, title, plot, char-acters names, setting, and interesting events in the book.
2. Begin framing the booktalk. Write captivating opening and closing lines. Include the information written down in step 1.

3. Select books that are appropriate for the developmental level of your students.
4. Create bookmarks or lists with the book information on them.

Creating a Hook

How will you generate interest in the titles you are talking? You need to use a hook. A hook is something that catches people's attention. Most songs have a catchy beat, chorus, or sing-along part. Think about commercials. What technique do they use to get us to remember them?

What Are Possible Hooks?

Change your voice and pattern of speech! Is there an accent used by a character that you could use?

Can you pretend to be the character? Teens especially respond to first-person booktalks.

Pretend the events of the story really happened to you!

Present the booktalk as an interview or as a news story.

More Hooks

Tell the story from the viewpoint of different characters.

Make it funny.

Build it around several cliffhangers that leave your audience wanting to know what happens next!

Find a phrase that fits to repeat throughout the booktalk.

Read a short passage that will get the students wanting to know more.

You can also create interest by having an introductory, concluding, or background piece of music that sets a mood.

The First Sentence

Make it count! Grab the audience's attention by:

- using a quotation or description of a character,
- focusing on a strong feeling,
- acting out an attention grabbing behavior,
- focusing on a shocking event, or
- relating to something the audience shares. For example, the first day of school, a family vacation, or an embarrassing moment.

The Last Sentence

Make it memorable!

If it fits, try to end with the title.

Use the same strategies for the opening sentence by creating some strong emotion or including something shocking.

Don't misrepresent the book, but try to pick out an exciting part of the book to highlight.

In general:

- Keep it simple by focusing on only a few characters and using short descriptive sentences.
- Even if you are reading a section from the book, practice it so you know exactly how you want to read it.
- Keep it short! You can do a lot of selling in about a minute. Four minutes should be about the maximum amount of time.
- Less is more!
- Remember to be responsible, and keep your behavior and language appropriate!
- Never give the ending away!

ADAPTING BOOKTALKS FROM OTHERS

Some of us feel more comfortable using booktalks created by others. Maybe you don't have much experience writing booktalks and want to see what other booktalkers have done. Maybe you are on a very short timeline and simply don't have time to write your own. Whatever the reason, feel free to use booktalks created by others. But be sure that you are comfortable with the booktalk. Remember, every booktalker has his/her own style. You may need to adapt existing booktalks to suit your audience, setting, and style.

Resources

Booktalks Quick and Simple: http://www.nancykeane.com/booktalks
Booktalking Colorado: http://booktalkingcolorado.ppld.org
Random House Booktalks: http://www.randomhouse.com/teachers/librarians/booktalks/booktalks.html
The Booktalker Booktalks by Joni Bodart: http://www.thebooktalker.com/archives.htm
TeensPoint Booktalks: http://www.teenspoint.org/reading_matters/booktalks.asp

PRESENTATION TIPS AND TRICKS

Once you have your booktalks written and your presentation planned out, it is time for the main event. Again, you need to create your own style. And that style may change based on the book you are talking. You don't want to be bouncy and bubbly when you are booktalking a sad book. Here are some good resources that give you some ideas for presentations.

Resources

How to Do a Book Talk by Gale Eaton: http://www.uri.edu/artsci/lsc/Faculty/geaton/MSLMAtalk
Connecting Young Adults and Libraries by Patrick Jones: http://members.aol.com/naughyde/connect.htm

How to Present Booktalks: http://web.archive.org/web/20041027200552/http://www.washburn.edu/mabee/crc/booktalks/howtobooktalk.html
Rah-Rah Reading! by Ellen A. Thompson: http://www.scholastic.com/librarians/ab/articles/rahrah.htm
Booktalking Tips and Tricks: http://www.nancykeane.com/booktalks/tips.htm

USING BIBLIOGRAPHIES AND BOOKLISTS TO SUPPORT BOOKTALKS

When preparing for an entire booktalk presentation, you should have a plan for what books you are showcasing. Are you working around a theme? Are you only talking one genre? Are you talking about award winners? To help you choose which books to include, it is helpful to consult booklists.

Resources

ATN Reading Lists wiki: http://atn-reading-lists.wikispaces.com
Newbery Winners: http://www.ala.org/ala/alsc/awardsscholarships/literaryawds/newberymedal/newberymedal.htm
Printz Winners: http://www.ala.org/ala/yalsa/booklistsawards/printzaward/Printz.cfm
Boston Globe-Horn Book Awards: http://www.hbook.com/bghb/default.asp
Database of Award-Winning Children's Literature / Lisa R. Bartle: http://www.dawcl.com
TeenReads: http://www.teenreads.com/reviews/index.asp
Booklists of Children's Literature compiled by MCPL: http://www.monroe.lib.in.us/childrens/booklists/children_booklists.html
Carol Hurst's Children's Literature Site: http://www.carolhurst.com/index.html
Booktalk! A Simple Way to Inspire Kids to Read: http://www.scholastic.com/bookfairs/books/booktalk.asp
Booktalking can open up a new world to middle and high school students By J. Marin Younker: http://www.schoollibraryjournal.com/article/CA6319896.html
"Talking" Books Creates a Hook!: http://www.education-world.com/a_curr/curr214.shtml
Book Talks by Denise Johnson: http://www.readingonline.org/electronic/elec_index.asp?HREF=webwatch/book_talks/index.html
Hartman, Maureen. Booktalks: Why these work, qualities of books for reluctant readers: http://media.mpls.k12.mn.us/sites/417ee2d6–0482–48ed-9621–9692f6b7bd7d/uploads/booklistmaureen2.pdf
Booktalking ideas: http://www.albany.edu/~dj2930/yabooktalking.html

RESEARCH FOR TECHNOLOGY WITH BOOKTALKS

Media Literacy is a 21st century approach to education. It provides a framework to access, analyze, evaluate and create messages in a variety of forms—from print to video to the Internet.

—Thoman & Jolls, 2005, p. 23

Having a research base can provide guidance for selecting from the many options or strategies that exist today. Booktalking with technology provides a strategy that incorporates a variety of strategies into the learning process. The National Reading Panel states that using a multiple strategy process for instruction is an effective way to achieve comprehension (National Institute of Child Health and Human Development, 2000). Booktalking would include the Panel's supported strategies of summarizing, comprehension monitoring, and cooperative learning. Use of multimedia and video technologies can improve reading comprehension and vocabulary for diverse learners in a variety of settings. Additionally, the use of technology can create a situation where students feel comfortable and where many students who might be too shy to participate in a face-to-face situation can participate comfortably (Beach & Lundell, 1998). Integrating carefully chosen technology applications that provide immediate student feedback and progress monitoring can be more effective than regular group instruction for a diverse range of students. The integration of technology tools can create a learning situation that provides its own feedback that will motivate learning and keep students cognitively engaged, especially when corrective feedback is provided (Goldenberg, Russell, & Carter, 1984). Integrating multimedia technology can also have a long-term effect on understanding and retention. For example, in a study of middle schoolers using a multimedia tool for learning, the immediate effects on the students were not different from those not using multimedia, but in terms of the long-term effects, a year later the students who had used multimedia displayed a greater grasp of the concepts and ideas (Lehrer, 1993). Technology can support cooperative learning and problem solving. Cooperative technology integration can result in improving daily achievement, increased retention of information, and higher level cognitive abilities including the application of information and problem solving (Bracewell, Breuleux, Laferriere, Beniot, & Abdous, 1998). In addition to the learning of content, there are consistent findings regarding improvement in student attitude and self-concept, as student attitudes toward learning and self-concept were both found to be consistently increased in a technology-rich environment (Sivin-Kachala & Bialo, 1994). Students don't just love the technology for itself; what they love about it is the freedom that it enables for their own expression and communication (New, 2007).

While most students may decide on what to read first from their own browsing, with teachers and library media specialists much further down in priority (Braeder, 1984), booktalking as a kind of advertising can have a positive effect on reading selection. For example, in a study of book circulation in an elementary school, researchers found that after a series of booktalks was presented, 80 percent of the students who checked out titles stated that booktalks were the primary motivating reason for checking out the book. The booktalk books were selected about twice as often as other available books (Nollen, 1992). Another study with adolescents found similar results: circulation of booktalk titles increased significantly after booktalk presentations. This effect occurred not only immediately after the booktalks but for an extended period of time after hearing the booktalks (Reeder, 1991).

REFERENCES

Beach, R., & Lundell, D. (1998). Early Adolescents' Use of Computer-Mediated Communication in Writing and Reading. In D. Reinking, M. C. McKenna, L. Labbo, and R. Kieffer

(Eds.), *Handbook of Literacy and Technology: Transformations in a Post-Typographic World* (Vol. 379, pp. 93–112). Mahwah, NJ: Lawrence Erlbaum Associates.

Bracewell, R., Breuleux, A., Laferriere, T., Beniot, J., & Abdous, M. (1998). *The Emerging Contribution of Online Resources and Tools to Classroom Learning and Teaching.* Montreal: University Laval. Retrieved March 19, 2002, from http://www.tact.fse.ulaval.ca/ang/html/review98.html.

Braeder, D. (1984). Booktalking: A Survey of Student Reaction. *Canadian Library Journal, 41,* 211–214.

Elley, W. B. (1992). *How in the World Do Students Read?* Hamburg: International Association for the Evaluation of Educational Achievement.

Goldenberg, E., Russell, S., & Carter, C. (1984). *Computers, Education and Special Needs.* Reading, MA: Addison-Wesley.

Krashen, S. (2004). *The Power of Reading: Second Edition: Insights from the Research.* Englewood, CO: Libraries Unlimited.

Lehrer, R. (1993). Authors of Knowledge: Patterns of Hypermedia Design. In S. P. Lajoie & S. J. Derry (Eds.), *Computers as Cognitive Tools.* Hillsdale, NJ: Lawrence Erlbaum.

National Institute of Child Health and Human Development (NICHD). (2000). *Teaching Children to Read: An Evidence-Based Assessment of the Scientific Research Literature on Reading and Its Implications for Reading Instruction: Reports of the Subgroups.* Report of the National Reading Panel (NIH Publication No. 00–4754). Washington, D.C.: U.S. Government Printing Office.

New Global Study From MTV, Nickelodeon and Microsoft Challenges Assumptions About Relationship Between Kids, Youth & Digital Technology. (2007). *News Release PR Newswire.* Retrieved July, 2007, from http://www.prnewswire.com/cgi-bin/stories.pl?ACCT=104&STORY=/www/story/07–24–2007/0004631532&EDATE=.

Nollen, T. D. (1992). *The Effect of Booktalks on the Development of Reading Attitudes and the Promotion of Individual Reading Choices.* PhD Dissertation, University of Nebraska—Lincoln. Retrieved November, 2005, from http://digitalcommons.unl.edu/dissertations/AAI9225488.

Reeder, G. M. (1991). *Effect of Booktalks on Adolescent Reading Attitudes.* PhD Dissertation, University of Nebraska—Lincoln. Retrieved November, 2005, from http://digitalcommons.unl.edu/dissertations/AAI9129570.

Scholastic. (2007). Harry Potter Books, Games, and Activities for Muggles. Retrieved July 25, 2007, from http://www.scholastic.com/harrypotter.

Sivin-Kachala, J., & Bialo, E. (1994). *Report on the Effectiveness of Technology in Schools, 1990–1994.* Washington DC: Software Publishers Association.

Thoman, E., & Jolls, T. (2005). *Literacy for the 21st Century.* Center for Media Literacy. Retrieved July, 2007, from http://www.medialit.org/pdf/mlk/01_MLKorientation.pdf.

2

Booktalk Technology

Students enjoy booktalks whether they are given by the teacher, library media specialists, or other students. Students can become booktalkers by simply talking about a book they liked. Students and educators can become tech-savvy booktalkers by adding some pizzazz into their presentation.

STANDARDS

Teachers are living and teaching in an age of standards. It seems that if there isn't a standard, then we shouldn't teach it, but don't let that stop anyone from having booktalks be part of their curriculum. Booktalks fit nicely into many subject areas and help introduce materials that meet a large number of different standards from a variety of topics. From library to literacy, from English Language Arts to technology, booktalks can be effective tools for standards-based learning and assessment. Booktalks even fit well with the No Child Left Behind Act (NCLB) in that it can be one of the reading comprehension strategies used as an essential component of reading instruction (U.S. Department of Education [DOE], 2007).

Booktalks are an excellent way to acquaint students and teachers with the American Association of School Librarian (AASL) standards for 21st-Century Learners (AASL, 2007). For example, integrating technology in a student-created booktalk could be used to meet the standard about organization and sharing of information (Standards 2.1.4, 2.1.6, 3.1.4, 4.1.6). Having students create their booktalks though multimedia tools would meet standards about creative development of products (Standards 3.3.4, 4.1.8). Having students share their booktalks in written form by posting to sites such as a blog or Amazon.com reviews could be an example of contributing to the learning society (Standards 1.1.9, 1.3.4, 2.1.5, 3.1.2, 3.2.2, 3.2.3, 3.3.1, 3.3.5, 4.3.1).

Depending on the type of technology being used by a student to create a booktalk, the creation of the booktalk with technology can meet a number of standards for language arts as put forth by the National Council of Teachers of English (NCTE) and the International Reading Association (IRA; NCTE & IRA, 1996). Any way that the students create and share their booktalks with others meets standards for effective forms of communication (Standards 4 & 7). A booktalk that includes images or other forms of multimedia would meet the standards for applying media techniques to discuss print (Standards 6 & 12). Creating a booktalk by using a presentation tool would have the student meeting the standards about synthesizing information, then creating and communicating interest in the book being read (Standard 8). Booktalks don't have to be done in isolation by the students: A booktalking project is a great opportunity for collaborative development either within the class or when sharing with the world (Standard 11).

By using technology in the creation of booktalks, in addition to subject area standards students are meeting a number of the National Educational Technology Standards for Students as identified by the International Society for Technology in Education (ISTE, 2007). By creating presentations, podcasts, or video students demonstrate creativity with technology in generating new products (Standard 1a). By placing their podcasts online or by creating videos and posting them to sites, such as YouTube or Google, they are publishing digital media for communication and collaboration (Standard 2a). As the creation of a technology-enhanced booktalk is not a quick thing to do, the students are engaged in long-term projects involving planning and managing their activities to complete the booktalk (Standard 4b). Because all these activities integrate technology the students constantly gain experiences with the technology operations and concepts as they use the resources (Standards 6a & 6b).

Although each state has its own educational standards that must be addressed, booktalking and using technology to enhance booktalking meets many common state standards. For example, based on the Florida Reading/Language Arts Standards for 11th and 12th grades (Florida DOE, 2007), when students develop and present their own technology-enhanced booktalks to a class or online they meet several standards including the following:

Reading Process

Reading Comprehension Standard: The student uses a variety of strategies to comprehend grade level text.

LA.1112.1.7.3—determine the main idea or essential message in grade-level or higher texts through inferring, paraphrasing, summarizing, and identifying relevant details and facts;

Writing

Prewriting Standard: The student will use prewriting strategies to generate ideas and formulate a plan.

LA.1112.3.1.2—making a plan for writing that addresses purpose, audience, a controlling idea, logical sequence, and time frame for completion;

Revising Standard: The student will revise and refine the draft for clarity and effectiveness.

LA.1112.3.3.1—evaluating the draft for development of ideas and content, logical organization, voice, point of view, word choice, and sentence variation;

Publishing Standard: The student will write a final product for the intended audience.

LA.1112.3.5.1—prepare writing using technology in a format appropriate to the purpose (e.g., for display, multimedia);

LA.1112.3.5.3—sharing with others, or submitting for publication.

Creative Standard: The student develops and demonstrates creative writing.

LA.1112.4.1.2—incorporate figurative language, emotions, gestures, rhythm, dialogue, characterization, plot, and appropriate format.

Persuasive Standard: The student develops and demonstrates persuasive writing that is used for the purpose of influencing the reader.

LA.1112.4.3.1—write essays that state a position or claim, present detailed evidence, examples, and reasoning to support effective arguments and emotional appeals, and acknowledge and refute opposing arguments;

Communication

Listening and Speaking Standard: The student effectively applies listening and speaking strategies.

LA.1112.5.2.2—apply oral communication skills in interviews, formal presentations, and impromptu situations according to designed rubric criteria;

LA.1112.5.2.3—use research and visual aids to deliver oral presentations that inform, persuade, or entertain, and evaluates one's own and others' oral presentations according to designed rubric criteria;

Information and Media Literacy

Media Literacy Standard: The student develops and demonstrates an understanding of media literacy as a life skill that is integral to informed decision making.

LA.1112.6.3.2—ethically use mass media and digital technology in assignments and presentations, citing sources according to standardized citation styles;

LA.1112.6.3.3—demonstrate the ability to select print and nonprint media appropriate for the purpose, occasion, and audience to develop into a formal presentation.

Technology Standard: The student develops the essential technology skills for using and understanding conventional and current tools, materials, and processes.

LA.1112.6.4.1—select and use appropriate available technologies (e.g., computer, digital camera) to enhance communication and achieve a purpose (e.g., video, presentations);

LA.112.6.4.2—routinely use digital tools for publication, communication, and productivity.

NEW LITERACIES

At one point in history *literacy* meant the ability to read words on paper, including books, newspapers, and job applications. In 1991, with the National Literacy Act, the

U.S. Congress redefined literacy as "an individual's ability to read, write, and speak in English, and compute and solve problems at levels of proficiency necessary to function on the job and in society, to achieve one's goals, and develop one's knowledge and potential" (National Institute for Literacy, 1991). Today, the concept of literacy seems to always be changing. Literacy now goes beyond paper to include reading from computers and personal devices. In addition, there are new literacies, such as media literacy, technology literacy, and information literacy (Semali, 2001).

The Internet and other forms of information and communication technology regularly redefine the nature of literacy. In order for a student to become fully literate in today's work, he or she must become proficient in these new and changing literacies. For example, the State Educational Technology Directors Association (SETDA) states that media literacy is an important part of today's literacy and that students should know "how to access, understand, analyze, evaluate, and create media messages on television, the Internet, and other outlets" safely, productively, and ethically (Stansbury, 2007). In a survey of states, concerning media literacy, it was found that although media may have many different names, the knowledge and skills that are part of this literacy are important, and effort is being made toward developing integrated standards (SETDA, 2007). Educators need to integrate technologies into today's literacy curriculum in order to prepare students for their literacy future.

THE DIGITAL STUDENT

Today's students are a group that uses communication technology and the Internet to stimulate their interest in learning. Using a technology-integrated approach to booktalks should help teachers to motivate their technology-integrated students. Today's generation of students, sometimes called *millennials*, includes nearly 50 million students in our schools today, representing the largest and most diverse group in our educational history (Patrick, 2004). These are students who have lived their whole lives with the Internet and its associated communication tools, and they love how it enables them to communicate at any time, to express themselves, and even to be entertained (New, 2007). For example, they prefer to find information in the Internet because they feel that the information is more abundant, accessible, and up-to-date (U.S. DOE, 2004). Just looking at how today's average high school students spends their time shows some of the differences from previous generations; today's students weekly spend more time on the Internet (16.7 hours) than watching television (13.6 hours), and they still find time for talking on the phone (7.7 hours; Yahoo!, 2003).

The world of our students is filled with new types of information, communication, presentation, and publication systems. Many students are already familiar with a variety of technology tools, while others are not. Unfortunately, many teachers are not as technologically literate as their students and may feel reluctant to use these tools with them. Additionally, schools may have limited or unreliable technological capacities. Even schools that have success at fostering high literacy for their students often don't include digital technologies such as hypertext, technology-based reading and writing, digital production, and other forms of technology integration. Students may feel that school is becoming very different from the outside world because most school students and the adult professional population use these valuable, technology-based communication and research tools on a daily basis, while classrooms don't (Meltzer, Smith, & Clark, 2001). On the other hand, there have been consistent findings regarding improvement in student attitudes toward learning and their self-concept in a technology-rich environment (Sivin-Kachala & Bialo, 1994). Integrating computer applications such as multimedia creation and presentation with booktalks allows for effective integration of technology for student success.

DIFFERENTIATED INSTRUCTION AND ACCOMMODATIONS

There is a wide range of educational needs among students in any classroom today, and there is a wide range of strategies for meeting them. Using booktalks can be an effective classroom strategy for differentiated instruction. The inclusion model of the classroom has become the norm. For the 2000–2001 school year, approximately 11.5 percent, 5.5 million students in grades K–12 in U.S. public schools, were classified as having some kind of disability (Koenig & Bachman, 2004). In addition, in 2004, over 10 percent, 5 million students, were identified as English as a second language learners (ESOL, ESL, LEP, etc.; National Clearinghouse for English Language Acquisition and Language Instructional Programs, 2004), and that number is only growing. One recognized effective method for teaching in classes with such a student population is differentiated instruction. Differentiated instruction is an educational approach to teaching and learning for students of differing abilities in the same class, with the intent to maximize growth and success while assisting in the learning process (Hall, n.d.). Integrating technology as part of a booktalk allows teachers to use a differentiated instruction model that recognizes that students have different background knowledge, readiness, language, learning styles, and interests.

According to Tomlinson (2001), teachers can differentiate three aspects of the curriculum or instruction: content, process, and products (Willis & Mann, 2000). Each of these three aspects of differentiation relates to the use of technology to create booktalks. *Content* refers to the concepts, principles, and skills that students are to learn and the strategies teachers use to provide students access to those skills and knowledge. Teachers can link interest-based exploration with their own key components of the curriculum and use skills or ideas that are already familiar to the student as a bridge to learning new ideas or skills. *Process* refers to the activities that students participate in where flexible grouping is used; these activities can be modified or provided with more scaffolding, depending on a student's readiness. Because of the possible complexity of some of the technology-enhanced booktalk projects and the different levels of skill and sensitivity each individual brings to their execution, teachers may make

Effective Differentiated Activity is something students will make or do:

- in a range of modes at varied degrees of sophistication in varying time spans
- with varied amounts of teacher or peer support (scaffolding)
- using an essential skill(s) and essential information
- to understand an essential idea/principle or answer an essential question.

(Tomlinson, 2001, p. 80)

them cooperative projects. *Products* refers to projects and materials that are created that demonstrate what students have learned and that different students can create different products based on their own readiness levels, interests, and learning style. For example, a student could create a blog, a podcast, or even a video, selecting the project topic based on skills and interests. An effective differentiated activity starts with an engaging activity, and booktalks are engaging activities for students.

CLASSROOM/TECHNOLOGY MANAGEMENT

Collaboration between the classroom teacher and the library media specialist provides a rich learning environment for the students. Each teacher brings his/her area of expertise to the project, and the students benefit from those areas of strength. The classroom teacher and the library media specialist should meet prior to the unit to discuss how the lesson will be taught and how classroom management will be handled.

There are a variety of strategies and methods for integrating technology with booktalking. The integration of technology with a booktalk can be done by a single student, a small group (such as a reading group from a literature circle), or a whole class, depending on the availability of the technology. The configuration of the technology will vary along with the management of how the students complete their booktalk activity. The configuration and management will change depending on the number and type of available computers and the grouping strategy. A teacher or school library media specialist working with a class could have the students create booktalks in the following ways.

- **Whole Class:** Have students self-select their reading. After finishing the reading, model how to develop and give a booktalk to the students. Once the students understand the process, have the whole class, either individual or in small groups, develop their technology-enhanced booktalks.
- **Small Group:** Group students with a common reading topic or book. Have the group complete their reading and then develop the outline of their booktalk. Provide access for the group to then produce their technology-enhanced booktalk.
- **Independent:** Have students individually read their assigned or selected readings. Provide students the option of creating a technology-enhanced booktalk as their reflective activity after reading.

CLASSROOM AND SCHOOL LIBRARY TECHNOLOGY CONFIGURATIONS

In school libraries and classrooms it is common to find a variety of computer situations that may mix desktop computers, laptops, or even handhelds. The computer configurations found in school rooms include the networked stand-alone single computer; the two to few computers, usually clustered in some part of the room; and the full computer lab design or portable lab (Cavanaugh, 2005). It is possible to integrate technology with booktalks in each of these configurations, from a one-computer situation to a full computer lab (see Figure 2.1).

Each of the different configurations provides different opportunities for the instructor and has its own limitations. For example, few computers available usually means less time that an individual student has with the technology in class.

While many may think that with a one-computer classroom it would not be possible for a class of students to effectively use technology in projects, consider that not everyone has to be doing exactly the same kind of thing always at the same time. The single computer in a classroom can be used by either a single student or small group that is cooperatively developing their booktalk. Here students can access a single computer to use multimedia creation or planning tools. To increase students' access to the technology for their booktalks, consider sharing one or two of your computers with other teachers or checking out com-

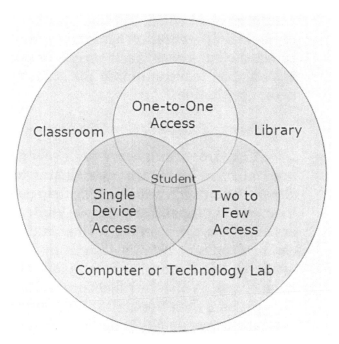

Figure 2.1. Technology access configurations that can be used in student-created booktalks.

puters or laptops from the school library. Often a computer can be put on a cart and shared among teachers. If the lesson is being carried out in the library media center, there will be more computers to accommodate students. Teacher teams and school librarians can also get together to share computers in a single room to create a technology center for student use or plan strategies for using the school library computers. As the access to technology increases for the students, so too will the options for integration.

Technology Management

It is important that teachers and library media specialists establish procedures to manage the technology resources and student access so that technology-integrated activities will flow smoothly, and every student gets access to the technology. The instructor should also check that all of the necessary equipment, batteries, software, and so forth are available and working.

One-to-One or Computer Labs

A lab—either as a part of the school media center, a separate room, or as a portable set of laptops, often available though the library—allows more students simultaneous access. There may be scheduling issues and time restraints limiting technology access. For instance, you may only be able to schedule the lab for a single day of the week. This does not mean that your students cannot create their technology-enhanced booktalks. The situation just necessitates additional planning. Instead of using the technology throughout the project, break up the project and have the students complete a number of activities "off line" (without computers). Students can complete a number of booktalk preparation activities without full access to computers. For example, they can create storyboards and scripts or take pictures with a digital camera. When the lab is available, make sure that the students are aware of the time restrictions and goals before beginning.

Two to Few or Several Computers

A classroom or library with several computers can serve as a learning center or booktalk development station. Instructors often find that having the computers in the classroom is much more flexible than using a computer lab (unless all the students have their own laptops). For example, students can save their projects on the center computers and then work on them later as time allows. In this configuration, the computers can be used on a rotational basis by individuals or groups. The number of computers available will determine how many rotations and the time each student or group will have access. While the others are waiting, they can do their own "off line" activities as they prepare their booktalks. Also, with multiple computers, teachers or library media specialists may decide to dedicate specific computers within the room for specific roles, such as one for creating audio booktalks, another for presentation software, and a third for video booktalks.

Single Device or One Computer

While it can be challenging to have students create technology-enhanced booktalks with one computer, it is possible. In addition to using the computer as a presentation tool for the completed booktalks, it can function as the development station for individuals or small groups. With one computer a rotational schedule should be developed for access, and while waiting, the off-computer students can be engaged in offline activities for their booktalk or other assignments. The computer can also be used by individuals or groups as a multimedia tool working with a scanner, a video camera, or a digital camera.

Scheduling Ideas

With either a single computer or a computer center students can be allocated amounts of time on a rotation schedule to use the computer or computers as they work on their booktalk project. It is important to discuss with your students how much time their project will take and to schedule them accordingly. It is always a good idea to also provide students with a step-by-step checklist and timeline with built-in checkpoints along the way. There are several strategies that an instructor can use to schedule time on the computers for individuals or groups. Keep in mind that students will need time away from the computer, such as for brainstorming, planning, and storyboarding. The following ideas can be used for scheduling and timing:

- Use a timer (such as an egg timer) and a student roster next to the computer. Have the students set the timer for 15 minutes and then tap the next person or group on the shoulder when their time is up.
- Post a schedule and have students or groups rotate at 15-minute shifts.

- Hang a string horizontally with labels on each end of "been there" or "not yet" above the computer (see Figure 2.2). Then write student or group names on clothespins and place them on the string. The labeled clothespins are placed to indicate whether the student or group has had their turn at using the computer that day.
- Use 3 x 5 cards or sticky note sheets color coded (for each weekday) with student names to identify computer users for each day; stick them on the wall next to the computer station. Students take turns cycling through the cards to complete their project.
- Create a weekly schedule and assign open blocks to students or groups.

Figure 2.2. Clothesline strategy of tracking turns for computer usage.

An additional aspect to account for in planning is students who may need help with the technology. One good assistance method is to have information reference sheets or posters of common usage steps to place near the computer stations. In addition, students can make effective volunteer computer assistants, coaches, or mentors. If students have a question or problem, they can ask the computer assistant for help, and if the assistant doesn't know, then s/he can ask the teacher. Instructors can have students working in groups with computer skills as a component for determining the group's makeup. The following are a few ideas from Intel (n.d.) that can be used by students who need assistance:

- *Flags:* Use colored flags on the computers or monitors. Yellow indicates help is needed, but the student can continue to work. A red flag signals an urgent issue, and the student cannot continue.
- *Cups:* Similar to the flags is to use colored cups nested upside down on the computer or monitor. Green on top for OK; yellow meaning assistance is

needed but student is still working; and red on top meaning the student needs help and can't continue.

Depending on students' abilities and experiences, students might need instruction for using removable media, network file storage, multimedia software, and available technology peripherals (such as scanners). Just because a room does not have full one-to-one computing options for all students doesn't mean that technology-based multimedia activities, such as booktalks, can't be done. For your students to be effective in creating their booktalk projects it is important that their instructors model effective and appropriate use of the technology as often as possible. Teachers should assess student projects in stages (outline, storyboard, narration script, etc.) instead of waiting until the end to evaluate the booktalk. Before starting any technology-integrated project, always have a back-up plan in case the technology crashes or is unavailable, and be prepared to do some troubleshooting of hardware and software (this is a good place for those student assistants). A school media specialist working with a teacher in assisting students to develop technology booktalks can make things much easier. The school librarian or media specialist can provide additional instruction, and the library may be able to also provide additional services. For example, if a classroom doesn't have a scanner, the library may. Through the teacher and librarian co-teaching a booktalking unit it is easier to identify resources and set-up schedules of how/when to use library and classroom computers-along with the additional resources available in the library so that things will go faster.

EDUCATOR COLLABORATION

Students, their teachers, and school library media specialists should all collaborate in the planning, development, and assessment of booktalks with technology. The library media specialist is an important team member who can explain the purpose of the booktalk and model several techniques and provide technology instruction, skills, and resources for students and teachers. The library media specialist should be involved with the planning of the project as well as the execution. Assessment can be carried out by the library media specialist and classroom teacher. In addition to identifying high-interest readings and assembling book collections, school library media specialists can make library computers and peripherals available for booktalk development or to promote the student- or teacher-created booktalks by creating associated displays and setting up a booktalk kiosk (see Chapter 9). Library media specialists can also organize space within the library media center, creating centers where students can present their booktalks to library visitors. Today, it is common for the school library media specialists to also edit the school Web space. Therefore, a library media specialist could also develop a school Web page to display the booktalks that students created.

Subject area teachers, school library media specialists, and the technology instructors can work together on technology-enhanced booktalking projects as interdisciplinary activities. In having students create booktalks, a language arts teacher may use the assignment as part of his/her curriculum for an activity/assessment in responding to literature. The technology or graphic arts instructor could then have the students use the booktalk as the topic where they create multimedia projects.

RESOURCES

Audio Excerpts

One way to entice students to read a book is to have them listen to a selection from the book. This can be accomplished by the teacher, library media specialist, or other students reading part of the book out loud as the booktalk. Research has shown that hearing text read aloud helps keep students engaged, it encourages students to read the books on their own, and "reading aloud to students has proven effective in secondary schools as well as in elementary schools" (Daye, 2003). Another strategy is to listen to the selection on audio. Hearing a good reader helps students develop fluency and the inner voice they need to fully comprehend text.

Audio clips of books are available over the Internet from several sources. The beauty of using these clips is that they are read by a professional reader. These professionals are trained in fluency and inflection to give the book the right presentation. Listening to these clips provides students with outstanding models for reading aloud and demonstrates how to give voice to characters. If you don't have access to the full audio book, just the short clip may be enough to get your students excited about reading the book.

In many of the audio book publisher online catalogs, the titles are accompanied by a short audio clip. The following online locations have audio excerpts:

Listening Library: http://www.randomhouse.com/audio
Blackstone Audio: http://www.blackstoneaudio.com
Full Cast Audio: http://www.fullcastaudio.com
Recorded Books LLC: http://www.recordedbooks.com
Simon & Schuster Audio Books: http://www.simonsays.com/content/index.cfm?pid=523076&tab=5
HarperCollins Audio: http://www.harpercollins.com/imprints/index.aspx?imprintid=517989

First Chapters and Excerpts

One way to get children to try a book is to have them read a few pages from the book. In a library setting, the library media specialists often suggest that the student read the first chapter or the first 10–20 pages to get a feel for the book. By using the technology available to us, this technique can be offered in several different ways.

1. Many automated library catalogs subscribe to a service from Syndetic Solution (http://www.syndetics.com). The subscription offers more than 178,000 first chapters and excerpts for prominently reviewed new titles, both fiction and nonfiction, and are available directly from the library public access catalog. Approximately 2,000 new chapters are added each month, and approximately 300 new excerpts are added each month. Excerpts include

poems, essays, recipes, forewords, and prefaces. *Check with your automation vendor to determine if your system supports this service.*

2. Many publishers offer excerpts of titles on their Web sites. These may be accompanied by author interviews. A few of the many that offer excerpts include:

Candlewick: http://www.candlewick.com
Farrar, Straus, Giroux: http://www.fsgbooks.com
Harcourt: http://www.harcourtbooks.com
HarperCollins: http://www.harperteen.com
Houghton Mifflin: http://www.houghtonmifflinbooks.com
Random House: http://www.randomhouse.com
Scholastic Books: http://www.scholastic.com
Simon & Schuster: http://www.simonsays.com

3. **Dear Reader:** http://www.dearreader.com

This site sends an e-mail every day that includes a 5-minute sample from a book. By the end of the week, you'll have read 2–3 chapters. The service mainly contains adult reads but also has a teen bookclub.

4. **Amazon.com:** http://www.amazon.com

Amazon offers Search Inside!™, which allows you to search millions of pages to find exactly the book you want to buy. With Search Inside!, search results include titles based on every word inside the book. Search Inside! results are displayed interspersed with results that match the title and/or author of the book. The Search Inside! feature also allows the student to view sample pages and read an excerpt of the book.

5. **Readers Read:** http://www.readersread.com/excerpts

Here you will find excerpts and first chapters from a variety of book genres including children's, fantasy, science fiction, mysteries, romance, and non-fiction.

6. **BookBrowse:** http://www.bookbrowse.com

Every week at BookBrowse you'll find an eclectic, informative and interesting selection of titles, from established writers to first time authors, from a wide range of genres, both fiction and non-fiction—so you can browse the cream of the crop without having to wade through shelves of also-rans. Mostly adult literature but includes some teen titles.

7. **Book Excerpts:** http://www.math.rutgers.edu/~sujith/bookexcerpts.html

A collection of extracts from several classic works of the 20th century.

8. **GMA Book Excerpts:** http://abcnews.go.com/GMA/Books

Mainly adult books but includes some titles appropriate for teens.

9. Free books on the Internet

The Online Books Page: http://digital.library.upenn.edu/books
This site offers a search engine that provides access to more than 18,000 listings of entire books freely available on the Internet (many of them older texts with expired copyrights). The site is hosted by the University of Pennsylvania Library and maintained by a digital library planner and researcher.
Bartleby.com: http://www.bartleby.com
This site offers free fiction and nonfiction books, short stories, poetry, and reference texts for research.
Project Gutenberg: http://www.gutenberg.org/wiki/Main_Page
This site aims to digitalize all books now in the public domain due to expired copyrights. Revisit the classics by William Shakespeare or Edgar Allan Poe or download a children's favorite such as *Alice in Wonderland*.
Children's Books Online: The Rosetta Project: http://childrensbookson line.org
The Rosetta Project offers free access to 90 illustrated children's classics such as *Peter Rabbit* and *The Three Bears*. Parents can download an entire book as a compressed zip file to store on the computer or to print out for bedtime stories. The site also offers books in multiple languages.
International Children's Digital Library (ICDL): http://www.icdlbooks.org
The ICDL is building an international collection and has over 1,600 titles online that reflects both the diversity and quality of children's literature from 38 countries and 42 languages (html, PDF).
Looky Book: http://www.lookybook.com
Allows you to look at picture books in their entirety—from cover to cover, at your own pace.

For listings of free online libraries visit http://www.drscavanaugh.org/ebooks.

DIGITAL STORYTELLING

When booktalking or using any technology in the classroom it is important to remember that the technology is secondary or supporting to the story being told. If you don't have a good booktalk to tell, using technology won't necessarily make it better (Banaszewski, 2002).

Creating digitally enhanced booktalks as a form of digital storytelling can be a valuable tool for learning because it can engage students in the learning process, develop decision-making skills, foster real-world connections, and encourage students to work collaboratively (Bransford, Brown, & Cockling, 2000; Kajder & Swenson, 2004; Levin, 2003; Simkins, Cole, Tavalin, & Means, 2002).

Stacy Behmer (2005), from her action research analysis, suggests four recommendations for successful technology-based presentations in classrooms.

1. Provide students with extended blocks of time to spend on this type of hands-on project-based learning activity.
2. Teach the technology skills within a meaningful context prior to the digital storytelling project.

3. Support teachers in classrooms as they use technology and assess its use.
4. Empower the students to take responsibility for the technology and their own learning.

Behmer (2005) concluded that the digital storytelling process, when implemented effectively, "has the potential to actively engage students in their own learning process. It is an authentic, hands-on learning experience, which utilizes multiple learning styles in a new way to address content and technology standards" (p. 53).

Students should ideally be selecting books and topics of interest to themselves for their booktalks, stories that they would like to research and share, which should improve the quality of the booktalks that they create. It is important to read the whole book before creating the booktalk because when you are telling someone else's story, it is important that you, as the booktalker, have enough information to fully understand the story, characters, and events (McDrury & Alterio, 2003).

Booktalking with technology provides an authentic experience because the students create and share their views, this sharing either in the development or delivery can have a notable impact on the quality of the student's work. As Bransford, Brown, and Cockling (2000) described, "Learners of all ages are more motivated when they can see usefulness of what they are learning and when they can use that information to do something that has an impact on others" (p. 61). When you create digitally enhanced booktalks and share them with a class or publish them on the Web, the students then are changing their role from being only a "learner" to "contributor," an aspect that makes this kind of digital project a more authentic learning experience (Levin, 2003). The video format of a booktalk, or digital booktalk is credited to Dr. Robert Kenny at the University of Central Florida's Digital Media Department. Dr. Kenny used video versions or trailers to introduce potential readers to books in 2004 (University of Central Florida, 2007).

Technology-integrated storytelling projects engage students both by addressing the needs of a diverse set of learners and because it is "hand-on." Strauss and Irvin (2000) found that effective literacy learning is flexible and responsive to students' diverse learning styles. Students' diverse learning styles and skill levels are applied as they use various forms of media to actively create their digital stories. The media technology students choose for their booktalk should also be based on their interests and how they want to share their story's booktalk. Even the opportunity for students to select "their" music raises their level of engagement and motivates students in their learning (Eggleton, 1995). Multimedia technology provides us with new ways to draw upon children's daily experiences with technology. According to Bracey (2002), we can expand the experiences of students with the use of today's multimedia because we have access to text, graphics, photos, animation, and video to draw upon their interests.

BOOKTALK TECH TOOLKIT

What are you going to need to create the technology-enhanced booktalks described in this book? This section will address some of that question. Part of that answer though will depend on the kind of booktalks you want to create and the computer that you have. For example, if you wanted to create live action video you would need some form of a video camera. To create a podcast booktalk you will need a microphone. The following items are some of the basic "tools" that you might want to have available. The components of this toolkit will allow users to create booktalks that can include text, images, narration, and soundtracks.

Hardware

There are a few devices that are useful for making your booktalks with technology, beyond the basic computer. You will most likely want some way to "take" images or pictures and a method for recording audio.

Computer

To make your technology-enhanced booktalks, you don't need a new top-of-the-line computer (although that does always help). Usually you can use one of the older multimedia machines. We would suggest (as of 2008) a Windows 2000 or Macintosh OS X operating system or above if possible. The issue is that the more multimedia you want to create the stronger a machine you will need. Be aware that the process of creating video can tax older systems.

While not actually part of the tool kit, you should also be thinking of the classroom setup for access and how you might be planning on using the technology with your class: individual access, small groups, or whole class.

In addition to the computer there will most likely be a few other items that booktalkers will find useful, including material for imaging and audio.

Imaging

For creating images, most people find either a digital camera or a scanner to be effective and easy tools. Neither is very expensive anymore, and both will connect to a computer to transfer images. Of the two, the camera may be the better, more flexible, option.

Digital Camera

Digital cameras have become quite common. The images are usually easily downloaded to a computer, using a USB cable and then imported for use in a variety of programs. These cameras are usually much faster at taking the "picture" as compared to using a scanner. Cameras can be used to help create the booktalks by taking pictures of student-created work, book covers, models, or even of students "acting" the parts.

In choosing a camera to use with a classroom there are a few recommendations:

1. *Batteries*—try to find a camera that uses a standard battery, such as a rechargeable AA or AAA, over one that requires a special proprietary battery. This way, if the batteries run down you can easily find a replacement instead of losing the use of the camera while the batteries recharge.
2. *Controls*—Point and Shoot. Find a camera that is simple to use, especially because it may be used by many students. Look for a camera with few and simple controls, and don't worry about special effects, controls, or conditions.

3. *Lenses*—Glass is best. Look for a camera that uses a glass lens. If you want a zoom feature, find a camera with an optical zoom, rather than a digital zoom. The optics make the camera, thus, a better lens makes a better camera. Students can also always zoom with their feet by walking up to the subject instead of zooming with the lenses.

4. *Storage Media*—Depending on your situation, consider the storage media for the files that will be created, such as flash cards. Look for storage that is simple and easy to put into the camera. Because the options vary in capacity, consider how many pictures your students will be taking for a project before they can be removed from the camera memory. An advantage of having a few storage cards is that with a card reader hooked to a computer some students can be working with the camera while others are working with their pictures on the computer.

5. *Flash*—Most cameras have a flash, but you might want to find one that has a control to turn the flash off.

6. *Video*—Most digital still cameras now also record video, so look for a camera that records video with sound (many don't). If students are adding narration, then the camera won't need to record sound with the video.

SOME OTHER RECOMMENDATIONS FOR YOUR CAMERA

Tripod—Find one that is rather small (6 inches) so it can sit on a desk. It has the added bonus of being easy to store.

Light—Use a simple desk or shop light.

Scanner

A scanner is another option for obtaining images, albeit it is slower to use than a camera. A simple flatbed scanner creates digital images of two- or three-dimensional objects placed against the scanning surface. If you are looking for a scanner, I would suggest that you choose one that runs from the USB port and doesn't require an external power source.

Audio

Adding the students' voice can be a powerful aspect of creating their booktalk. Two ways that students can capture their voices are to use a microphone with a classroom computer or to use a stand-alone digital recorder.

Microphone

A microphone connected to a computer may be the easiest classroom solution. At a minimum, we suggest that students use a wearable microphone, such as a headset microphone. While desktop stick microphones or microphones built-in to the computer's monitor can work, the quality caused by the distance between the person speaking and the microphone is often not very good. This decrease of sound quality is especially noticeable and becomes a problem as the students' move around or face different directions. Also, stick or monitor microphones are more likely to pick up ambient room noises in addition to the person speaking. At the high end, for an activity such as a group doing podcasting, a higher quality microphone, such as the Snowball, is a good selection. *See Chapter 7 for more information on microphones.*

Digital Recorder

Another option for voice recording is a digital recorder. Many mp3 players are also digital audio recorders. This device is an effective way to record student audio without a computer. Look for a recorder/player that can record audio in a common format, such as WAV or mp3, which can then be imported into your computer.

Software

The software being discussed here is in relation to working with the hardware discussed previously. The kind of booktalks you are creating will determine the kind of software needed. For example, if you or your students are interested in creating booktalks through standard podcasting, then imaging or presentation software will not be needed, but audio software is a must. We suggest that you begin with software that you already have or try reputable free, inexpensive, or open source software before you purchase more expensive versions of software. By starting with the free or public domain software you can identify the needs, options, and necessary skills before upgrading to more expensive software.

The software that you need depends on what you or your students are interested in creating. Some of the basic categories of software to consider include image manipulation, audio creation, and presentation. Some suggestions for each category include:

Image Manipulation

Paint or its equivalent—this is the standard image software program built into the operating system.

GIMP (www.gimp.com)—this is an open source program similar in function to PhotoShop (PC, Mac, Linux).

PhotoShop Elements—a relatively easy-to-use and inexpensive version of PhotoShop with most of the most-used aspects (PC, Mac).

Audio

Audacity (www.Audacity.com)—Open source presentation audio editing and creation software that can develop multitrack sounds and then mix them together (PC, Mac, Linux).

Garage Band—Apple's audio software that is great at creating enhanced podcasts (Mac).

Presentation

Inspire (www.OpenOffice.com)—Open source presentation software that is part of the Open Office Suite and can work with and create PowerPoint presentations (PC, Mac, Linux).

PowerPoint—One of the classic and best-known presentation programs (PC, Mac).

Video

Photo Story—An easy-to-use program that creates excellent video from still images (PC).

Movie Maker—Basic video editing software that is built in to most new systems (PC).

iMovie—Basic video editing software that is built in to most new systems (Mac).

REFERENCES

American Association of School Librarians (AASL). (2007). AASL Standards for the 21st-Century Learner. Retrieved May 3, 2008, from http://www.ala.org/ala/aasl/aaslproftools/learningstandards/AASL_Learning_Standards_2007.pdf.

Banaszewski, T. (2002, January/February). Digital Storytelling Finds Its Place In the Classroom. *Multimedia Schools.* Retrieved November 12, 2004, from http://www.infotoday.com/MMSchools/jan02/banaszewski.htm.

Behmer, S. (2005). Digital Storytelling: Examining the Process with Middle School Students. Retrieved February 15, 2007, from http://projects.educ.iastate.edu/~ds/Behmer/AReflection.doc.

Bracey, B. (2002). Extending the Information Revolution with Digital Equity and Inclusion. In S. Armstrong (Ed.), *Snapshots! Educational insights from the Thornburg Center* (pp. 21–31). Lake Barrington, IL: The Thornburg Center.

Bransford, J., Brown, A., & Cocking, R. (Eds). (2000). *How People Learn: Brain, Mind, Experience, and School.* Washington, D.C.: National Academy Press.

Cavanaugh, C. (2005). *Clips from the Classroom: Learning with Technology.* Upper Saddle River, NJ: Prentice Hall.

Daye, T. J. (2003). Read-Aloud—Research Briefs. Retrieved October 20, 2004, from, http://www.ncpublicschools.org/schoolimprovement/effective/briefs/readaloud?.

Eggleton, P. (1995). Motivation: A Key to Effective Teaching. *The Math Educator, 3*(2). Retrieved February 26, 2007, from http://math.coe.uga.edu/tme/issues/v03n2/Eggleton.pdf.

Florida Department of Education (DOE). (2007). New Reading and Language Arts Standards with Access Points. Retrieved December 31, 2007 from http://etc.usf.edu/flstandards/la/index.html.

Hall, T. (n.d.). Differentiated Instruction. CAST. Retrieved May 5, 2005, from http://www.cast.org/publications/ncac/ncac_diffinstruc.html.

Intel. (n.d.). Managing Computer Use: Challenges and Solutions. Retrieved August 1, 2007, from http://www.intel.com/education/newtotech/managing.htm.

International Society for Technology in Education (ISTE). (2007). National Educational Technology Standards for Students: The Next Generation. Retrieved September 2, 2007, from http://www.iste.org/Content/NavigationMenu/NETS/NETSforStudentsStandards2007.doc.

Kajder, S., & Swenson, J. (2004). Digital Images in the Language Arts Classroom. *Learning and Leading with Technology,* 31 (8), 18–21.

Koenig, J. A., & Bachman, L. F. (2004). Keeping Score for All: The Effects of Inclusion and Accommodation Policies on Large-Scale Educational Assessment. Board on Testing and Assessment Center for Education. Washington, D.C.: The National Academies Press.

Levin, H. (2003). Making History Come Alive. *Learning and Leading with Technology, 31*(3), 22–27.

McDrury, J., & Alterio, M. (2003). *Learning Through Storytelling in Higher Education.* Sterling, VA: Kogan Page Limited.

Meltzer, J., Smith, N. C., & Clark, H. (2001). Adolescent Literacy Resources: Linking Research and Practice. LAB at Brown University. Retrieved April 4, 2005, from http://www.alliance. brown.edu/pubs/adlit/alr_lrp.pdf.

National Clearinghouse for English Language Acquisition and Language Instructional Programs. (2004). 2002–2003 NCELA Poster. Retrieved June, 2004, from http://www.ncela. gwu.edu/policy/states/reports/statedata/2002LEP/Growing_LEP0203.pdf.

National Council of Teachers of English and the International Reading Association (NCTE & IRA). (1996). Standards for the English Language Arts. Retrieved July 20, 2007, from http://www.ncte.org/about/over/positions/category/stand/119263.htm.

"National Literacy Act of 1991." National Institute for Literacy. Retrieved July 21, 2007, from http://www.nifl.gov/public-law.html.

New Global Study From MTV, Nickelodeon and Microsoft Challenges Assumptions About Relationship Between Kids, Youth & Digital Technology. (2007). *News Release PR Newswire.* Retrieved July 25, 2007, from http://www.prnewswire.com/cgi-bin/stories.pl? ACCT=104&STORY=/www/story/07–24–2007/0004631532&EDATE=.

Patrick, S. (2004). The Millennials. Excerpted from a speech presented at the No Child Left Behind eLearning Summit, Orlando, Florida, July 13.

Semali, Ladislaus. (2001). Defining New Literacies in Curricular Practice. *Reading Online.* Retrieved July 12, 2007, from http://www.readingonline.org/newliteracies/semali1/index. html.

Simkins, M., Cole, K., Tavalin, F., & Means, B. (2002). *Increasing Student Learning Through Multimedia Projects.* Alexandria, VA: Association for Supervision and Curriculum Development.

Sivin-Kachala, J., & Bialo, E. (1994). *Report on the Effectiveness of Technology in Schools, 1990–1994.* Washington, D.C.: Software Publishers Association.

Stansbury, M. (2007). Groups Push for Media-Literacy Education. *eSchool News Online.* Retrieved July 12, 2007, from http://www.eschoolnews.com/news/showstoryts.cfm? Articleid=7252.

State Educational Technology Directors Association (SETDA). (2007). Leadership Summit Toolkit 2007. Retrieved July 12, 2007, from http://setda.org/web/guest/toolkit2007/ medialiteracy.

Strauss, S. E., & Irvin, J. L. (2000, September). Exemplary Literacy Learning Programs. What Research Says. *Middle School Journal, 32*(1), 56–59.

Tomlinson, C. A. (2001). *How to Differentiate Instruction in Mixed-Ability Classrooms,* 2nd ed. Alexandria, VA: Association for Supervision and Curriculum Development.

University of Central Florida. (2007). Digital Booktalk. Retrieved March 20, 2008, from http:// www.digitalbooktalk.com.

U.S. Department of Education (DOE). (2007). Reading—Proven Methods—No Child Left Behind. Retrieved July 31, 2007, from http://www.ed.gov/nclb/methods/reading/edpicks. jhtml?src=az.

U.S. Department of Education (DOE), Office of Educational Technology (OET). (2004). Toward a New Golden Age in American Education: How the Internet, the Law and Today's Students Are Revolutionizing Expectations. Washington, D.C.: Author. Retrieved April 4, 2005, from http://www.ed.gov/about/offices/list/os/technology/plan/2004/plan.pdf.

Willis, S., & Mann, L. (2000). Differentiating Instruction: Finding Manageable Ways to Meet Individual Needs. Curriculum Update. Retrieved May 30, 2005, from http://www.ascd.org/ed_topics/cu2000win_willis.html.

Yahoo!. (2003). Born to be Wired: Understanding the First Wired Generation. Retrieved August 12, 2006, from http://us.i1.yimg.com/us.yimg.com/i/promo/btbw_2003/btbw_execsum.pdf.

3

Text-Based Booktalks

This chapter examines the application of text publication technology and how it is used by students for creating and sharing booktalks. Online logs and journals can be used by a single student, a few students, or even a whole class depending on the needs of the students and the availability or access to technology.

IN THE CLASSROOM

James, a tenth-grade student in Mr. Ponti's language arts class, was using his word processor to complete his booktalk outline. While he had participated in classroom booktalks before, this one went further than a presentation to the class. In this assignment James was going to present his booktalk to the world by posting it to Amazon.com. As part of their sustained silent reading time, he and the whole class were able to choose a book that they liked and, after finishing their books, were assigned to present booktalks to the rest of the class based on their reading. What James found interesting and exciting was going beyond the standard book report or presentation to share his thoughts and ideas through the Internet. The book that James had chosen to read was Steven Gould's *Wildside* and, while he knew that he was going to give the book a five star rating, he was having trouble keeping all that he wanted to say about the book within the 1,000-word limit while still sharing his excitement about the book.

During the previous weeks, Mr. Ponti, working in collaboration with the school library media specialist, had presented a number of booktalks as examples to his class and had reviewed the parameters of the assignment. Now students were at various stages of completing the writing of their booktalks. Mr. Ponti felt that his students were more engaged and had a much more positive outlook on the reading assignment than they had with previous book assignments. Instead of being a standard paper or test, this assignment introduced his students to using Web 2.0 collaborative tools as they wrote their opinions and shared them beyond the classroom. Mr. Ponti felt that by sharing outside of the school, his students had improved attitudes and notable improvement in the quality of their final work.

Mr. Ponti teaches in a suburban school, and his classes are normally composed of 25 to 30 students. His classroom has the standard technology equipment for his school district, including four student desk computers and one laptop for the instructor (see Figure 3.1). Working with the school media specialist, Mr. Ponti has access to the school's

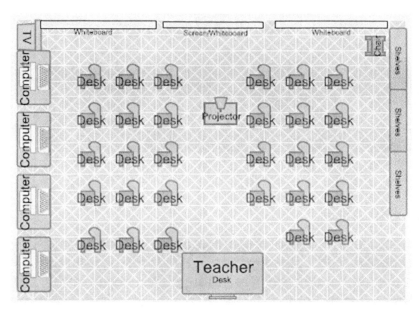

Figure 3.1. Mr. Ponti's classroom setup.

set of 10 Alphasmart Neos, which are writing keyboards. To overcome his classroom's lack of one-to-one computing, students were instructed to first write outline drafts on paper concerning their books. Then 10 students used the Neos to write their booktalks, while 4 more used the classroom computers. The teacher's laptop was always available for students who were using the Alphasmart Neos so they could transfer their files for printing, their final review, or to save onto the student's key drive. When a student had a complete booktalk, she went online to Amazon.com to post it on the book's page. The students also included their ratings of the books they read. Students printed their submissions for grading and then used the Web site and a video projector to present their booktalks to the class during the next week.

SAMPLE WRITING LESSON PLAN

Title: Amazonian Booktalk

Subject(s): English, language arts/reading

Grade level(s): Grade 9, High School (9–12)

Purpose/Outcomes/Objectives:

> To analyze a novel/story and write a concise booktalk to publish on the Internet.

> From their reading, students will analyze plot, character, content, style, form, and intended impact.

> Students will write reviews of their books in the form of a booktalk.

> Each student will use word processing to write, edit, copy, paste, and publish on the Internet.

Standards Addressed:

AASL

> 1.3.4 Contribute to the exchange of ideas within the learning community.

> 2.1.6 Use the writing process, media, and visual literacy and technology skills to create products that express new understandings.

3.1.2 Participate and collaborate as members of a social and intellectual network of learners.

4.1.7 Use social networks and information tools to gather and share information. (AASL, 2007)

State (Example—Florida)

LA.B. 1.4.3: The student uses writing processes effectively. Produces final documents that have been edited.

LA.B. 2.4.4: The student writes to communicate ideas and information effectively. Selects and uses a variety of electronic media, such as the Internet, information services, and desktop publishing software programs, to create, revise, retrieve, and verify information.

LA.A. 1.4.4: The student uses the reading process effectively. Applies a variety of response strategies, including rereading, note taking, summarizing, outlining, writing a formal report, and relating what is read to his or her own experiences and feelings.

Materials:

Novels/books to read. Books used can be chosen and read by individuals, groups (such as literature circles), or the whole class.

Active Amazon.com account will be needed

Computers with Internet access

Word processing software (such as MS Word)

Duration/length of the activity:

Two to three 45-minute class sessions

Prior Knowledge:

Each student should understand the parameters of a booktalk and have completed reading the book of his/her choice.

Review *General Review Writing Guidelines* from Amazon.com.

Procedures for conducting the activity:

(Day 0) Homework: write a rough draft of a booktalk.

(Day 1) After reading his/her book, each student will write a booktalk using word processing software. *Note: Max length for the booktalk is 1,000 words.*

(Day 1–2) This booktalk will be proofed and revised as often as necessary.

(Day 2) When it is ready to be published, the student will use Amazon.com to publish the booktalk electronically *(students can enter their review using the "Kid's Review" form).*

(Day 3) As an extension students can also publish locally by making a book-talk poster or book jacket to be displayed in the school library and or classroom. The poster can be made by using oversized sheets of paper (such as legal sized). They should add pictures, title and author, and quotes from their booktalk.

Putting the Booktalk on Amazon.com

1. Connect to the Internet using a Web browser program.
2. In the address section, type in **http://www.amazon.com.**
3. Make sure that the search is narrowed to "Books."
4. In the space to the right of "Book" write the name of the novel you will be reviewing.
5. Click on the "Write your own review" button, this will open a new page for submitting your review (booktalk).

Option: Select the link at the top of the page for "Use our Kids' Review Form."

6. Switch to or start your word processing program (e.g., MS Word).
7. Open your booktalk in the word processor.
8. Highlight/select your entire document and then from the Edit menu choose the option for Copy.
9. Switch back to the Internet browser (at Amazon.com).
10. Rate the book by assigning it a number of stars from 1–5.
11. In the "Please enter a title for your review" box, write a brief title for your booktalk, and add your initials.
12. In the "Type your review in the space below:" box, paste your booktalk from the word processor.
13. Select the "Preview your review" button to check your booktalk. If you see any mistakes then select the button to "Edit."
14. If everything about your booktalk looks as you want it, please print out a copy to submit to the teacher, and then select the button to "Save." Be sure to check your project against the assessment rubric (Table 3.1)

Assessment

Table 3.1
Classroom Setup

Area	3	2	1
Written Copy (word processed)	The student turns in hardcopy of the booktalk from online.	The student turns in a hardcopy of the booktalk, but not from online.	The student turns in a hand-written copy of the booktalk.
Length	Under 1,000 words		
Sequence	Begins with an interesting hook and then retells an exciting part of the story. The booktalk includes: title, author, and a personal reason for reading the book.	Begins by telling one or two details from story. The booktalk includes title and author.	The booktalk tells the entire story.
Setting	Many vivid, descriptive words are used to describe setting.	Word choices are limited, vague, or overused.	Reader would have a difficult time determining when and where the story takes place.
Characters	The main characters are named and described.	The main characters are named, but little description is provided	Hard to determine who the main characters are.
Problem/Plot	Story problem/plot is described, but ending is not told.	Problem/plot is described but hard to understand.	Problem/plot is unclear, or ending is told.

Writing with Technology

It is important to have students incorporate technology as part of their writing process. As Jeff Wilhelm (2000), discussing Bolter's (1991) research, suggests, "if our students are not reading and composing with various electronic technologies, then they are illiterate…right now" (p. 4). Most of today's students will need no instruction concerning the use of communication technology, and instead can be quite useful in teaching the teachers. It has become difficult to find many students who have not communicated using text messaging, e-mail, and chat or blogs. Recent studies have found that 96 percent of teens with Internet access use social networking tools, and some of the most common topics of discussion are education and schoolwork (National School Boards Association, 2007).

Writing in an online format can provide students with an expanded experience because they will write for their immediate classmates but also for the world at large. Students have a variety of online applications with which they can write their booktalks.

Some of the online applications include discussion forums, Weblogs or blogs, and other book sites, such as Amazon.com (see this chapter's lesson plan). Each of these applications allows a student to write using an online tool.

Using the computer offers additional benefits for building students' abilities. Kamil (2003), in reporting on research findings of the effects of computer communications on reading and writing, stated that students' written communications were found to improve in quality. These technologies, therefore, have been found to be effective and motivating to many students and are often part of their lives outside the school.

A Pew Internet & American Life Project report stated that 7 percent of adult Internet users in the United States have created blogs (Lenhart, Horrigan, & Fallows, 2004), with overall blog readership up 58 percent in one year. Teens are estimated to be approximately half of all blog creators. While many students are using blogs and other forms of interactive communication tools on the Internet to socialize, the potential exists for using them in classrooms as productive, high interest, collaborative tools for learning. Using these tools students can create and submit their booktalks to book discussion sites, such as Nancy Keane's Booktalks (http://nancykeane.com/booktalks/), or to a blogging site, such as one that was created for a school by a teacher or library media specialist. Additionally, teachers can go online to find other teachers to be club partners and have students from different classes post their own book reviews and discuss books.

It is important to integrate technology-enhanced writing activities, such as the one described, into the students' curriculum so that the students understand the value of online authoring for learning. Students can write assessments during class or as part of homework. Students may turn in printouts of their postings or instructors can request that students submit links so that instructors can read what the students have written online. Be sure to specify a time frame or deadline for the booktalk posting.

BLOG SITES

Blog hosting sites on the Web have become very popular. Some common free online blog sites include:

Blogger: http://www.blogger.com/
A service from Google that provides tools for publishing individual blogs.
Bloglines: http://www.bloglines.com/
A service from *Ask* that provides tools for publishing individual blogs.
BlogMeister *by David Warlick:* http://landmark-project.com/blogmeister/
A site where teachers can set up a password-protected class site for students.

Sites That Accept Booktalks

The Web 2.0 or the collaborative, social, read/write Web is an important part of what the Internet is used for today. No longer are people going online only to read what others have posted; today, collaborative sites make it possible to create content for the Internet. There are a number of places online where students can write up their own booktalks and post them for others to read. For example in Nancy Keane's *Booktalks Quick and Simple* (http://www.nancykeane.com/booktalks) there is a link to an online submissions form (see Figure 3.2). Here a student can write a booktalk and post it with the school name and his/her own first name. Other sites do not specifically focus on booktalks but do accept reviews and descriptions of books from students (aka booktalks). Sites such as *Amazon* or *Shelfari* may require an adult (such as the teacher, librarian, or school media specialist) to log in for the student to post a booktalk.

Sites to consider for student-posted booktalks:

Amazon: http://www. amazon.com

Barnes & Noble: http://www.bn.com

ePals Book Club: http://www.epals.com/projects/book_club

Genrefluent: http://www.genrefluent.com

LibraryThing: http://www.librarything.com

Nancy Keane's Book Talks—Quick and Simple: http://nancykeane.com/booktalks

Scholastic Share What You're Reading: http://teacher.scholastic.com/activities/swyar/index.asp

SeeMe4Books: http://www.seeme4books.com

Shelfari: http://www.shelfari.com

Spaghetti Book Reviews: http://www.spaghettibookclub.org

Teen Ink: http://teenink.com/Books

YARA Read a Review: http://www.yara-online.org/main_pages/read_review.htm *Note: This is a site from Australia.*

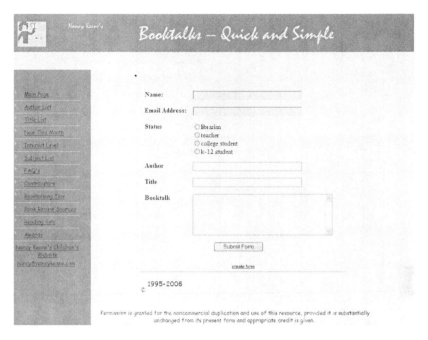

Figure 3.2. Nancy Keane's Booktalks Quick and Simple online submissions form (http://www.nancykeane.com/booktalks). Copyright © Nancy Keane 2007.

CREATING BOOKTALKS WITH BLOGS

Definition: Blog/WebLog: a Web page containing brief, chronologically arranged items of information. A blog can take the form of a diary, journal, what's new page, or links to other Web sites

From an education perspective the availability and ease of use of blogging software makes creating blogs a viable classroom activity and a means for teachers and library media specialists to share books and book discussions. Blogs not only provide a place to write, but readers can comment on what has been said. Blogs can also include links to Web sites, other blogs, news articles, or even pictures. Blog authors can also "tag" the entries with keywords. This makes it easier for others to find and share blog entries of interest.

Figure 3.3. Google's Blogger site for creating blogs (Weblogs). Copyright © Google 2007.

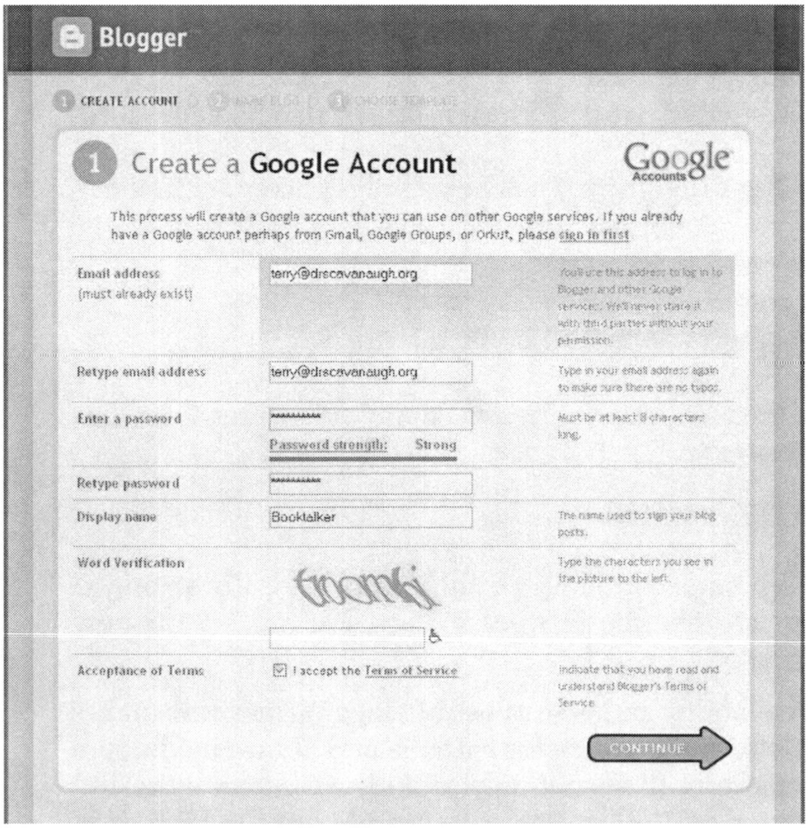

Figure 3.4. Creating an account with Blogger. Copyright © Google 2007.

One freely available blog hosting site is Blogger.com. Blogger is designed for the general public by Google. The following are step-by-step instructions for creating a blog with Blogger, which can be used to host school-created booktalks.

Go to the Blogger blog creation page (http://www.blogger.com/start) and click on the **Create your Blog Now** arrow (see Figure 3.3).

Here creating your blog is a relatively easy process of three basic steps.

Step 1: Create Your Blog Account

To create your account you will need a user name to sign in and add material to your blog, a password to prevent others from unauthorized adding, and a display name to establish your account. Complete the online form and then click on the **continue** arrow (see Figure 3.4).

Step 2: Name Your Blog

Next name your blog. Start by writing your title. For example, you could call your blog by your school or class name with the term *booktalk*. Then consider what you want the URL name to be. This will be the address people type in to view the blog. You can add a term to the name, but remember that there can be no spaces (although you could use characters such as dashes). Then you will need to check on whether that name is available. Once you have a name, fill in the security code (this makes sure that there is a person doing this and not a machine).

Then click on the **continue** arrow (see Figure 3.5).

Step 3: Choose Your Template

Now you will decide on how your booktalking blog will look. Instead of having to do all the design work, Blogger lets you choose a template. Review the available templates and then select the one you like the best for your blog.

Then click on the **continue** arrow (see Figure 3.6).

Now you have a blog! Click on the **Start Posting** arrow to go to your blog page. But before you start posting your own booktalks it is a good idea to review the settings and make a few decisions about how you want the blog to work.

Settings for Your Blog

Take the time to look at each of the options in the settings menu and either add the requested information or choose from the available settings (see Figure 3.7). Remember to click on the save settings for each page.

Post to Your Blog

Once your settings are complete, you can start blogging by posting. Begin by adding an

Figure 3.5. Naming your blog in Blogger. Copyright © Google 2007.

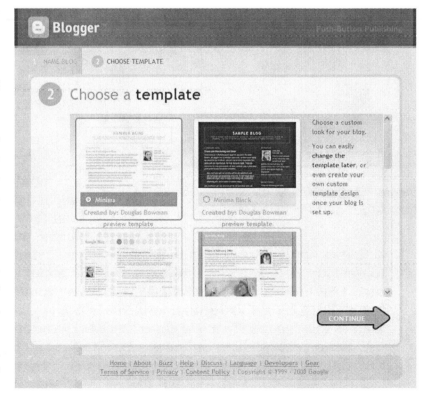

Figure 3.6. Selecting a template for a blog in Blogger. Copyright © Google 2007.

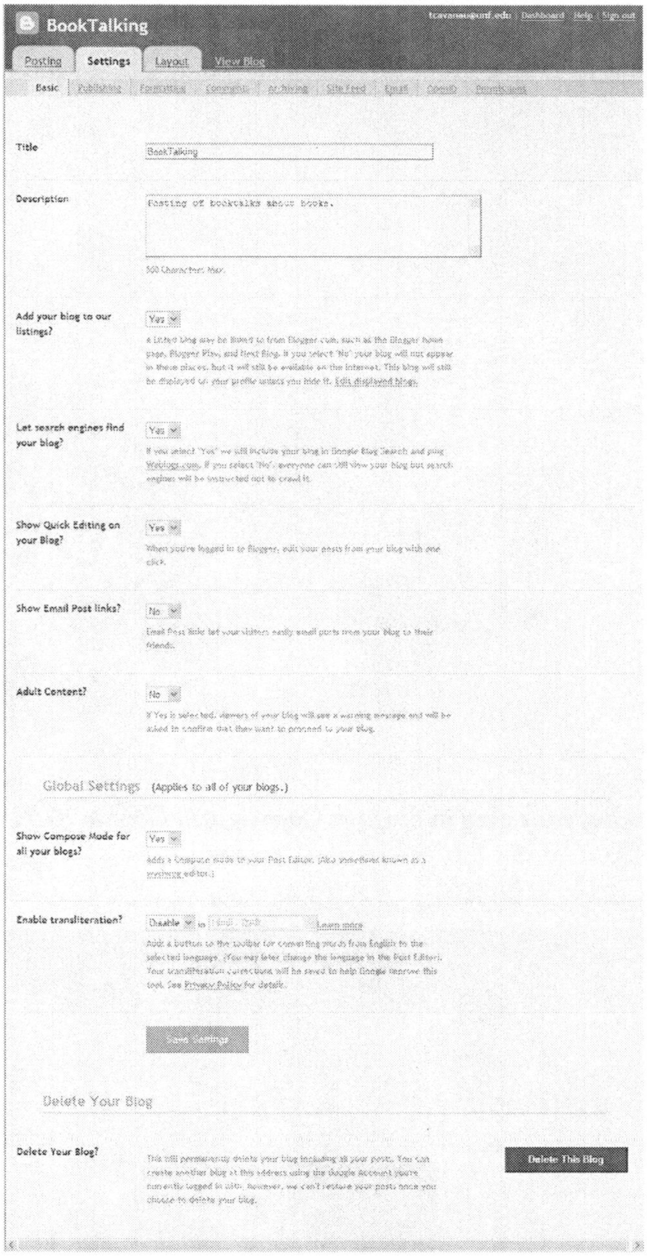

Figure 3.7. Completing the settings for the booktalk blog. Copyright © Google 2007.

introductory post to your blog, perhaps to describe the purpose of the blog or information about who will be posting. Then click on the **Publish Post** button (see Figure 3.8).

Step 4: Posting a Booktalk

Now that your blog is setup, it can be used to post the booktalks. The instructor will need to sign in if you are creating a account to be used by a class. Select the option to create a New Post. Add the book's title and author(s) to the subject line, and write in the booktalk in the larger text box (see Figure 3.9).

In the post it is possible to add images. Images, such as a book cover for the booktalk, can be uploaded from the computer being used for the writing or linked to from an online location and then positioned within the blog (see Figure 3.10). Often book covers are posted on the publisher's Web site, or they can be found at online book stores such as Amazon. Copy the Web address (URL) of the book cover and paste it into the URL blank.

The following is an example of a booktalk blog in Blogger (see Figure 3.11). This blog uses the school mascot as the blog's poster to entice students to read.

CARTOONING BOOKTALKS

Students can become bored by responding in the same ways to the books or stories that they read. Think about how many different multiple intelligences your current activities apply. It may help to improve interest, motivation, and student participation to develop new ways for students to think about or share literary works they have read. One effective alternative may be creating comic strips or cartoon squares for their booktalks. Using this format, students can analyze the plot, characters, events, and themes they've read in a few short scenes of a cartoon.

For some excellent online examples of comic booktalks visit the *Unshelved Book Club* (http://www.overduemedia.com/bookclub.aspx) to see close to 100 different booktalks by Gene Ambaum and Bill Barnes (see Figure 3.12).

Booktalk Cartooning Activity Steps

Before having students create their own comic booktalks, the instructor should select, review, and demonstrate to the class the Web site or software program that will be used to create the cartoon. Alternatively, students can browse among the Web sites or programs available to make their own selection.

To make booktalking comic strips in the classroom, some suggested steps and elements include:

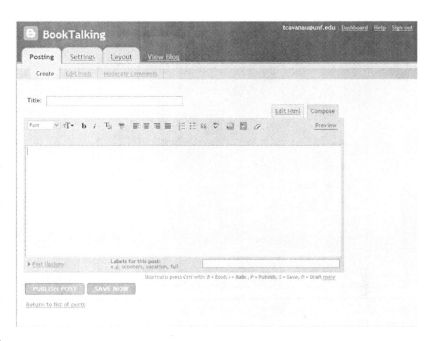

Figure 3.8. Creating a new post in Blogger. Copyright © Google 2007.

- The author and title of the book or story.
- The student name or group member names.
- For the number of frames selected (one, three, six, etc.) there should be images that either relate to or discuss elements of the story.
- Each frame should have a written caption.
- When finished, print three copies of your comic booktalk: one for the teacher, one for the library media specialists, and one for the student.

A complete lesson plan from Read-Write-Think on using Comic Strips for book reports is available at (http://www.readwritethink. org/lessons/lesson_view. asp?id=195) *and includes planning sheets and a comic strip rubric.*

For more information on using comics in the classroom visit NACAE—The National Association of Comics Art Educators (http://www.teachingcomics. org) *for resources including guides, suggested books, syllabi, and resource links.*

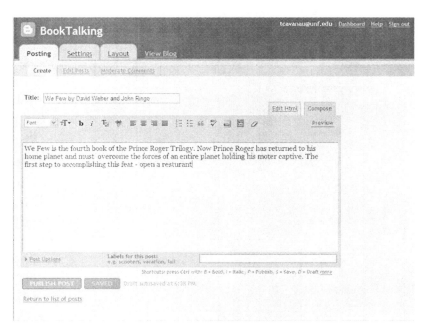

Figure 3.9. Beginning to write a booktalk post in Blogger. Copyright © Google 2007.

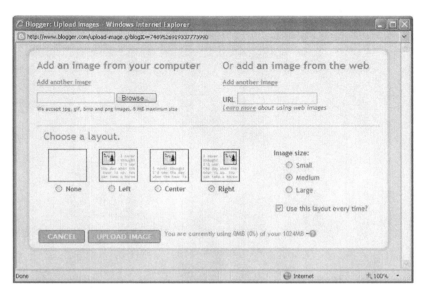

Figure 3.10. Adding images to the blog posting. Copyright © Google 2007.

Note: Create comic strips using photos from the Flickr Web site.

- **Comeeko.com**—http://www.comeeko.com
- **ComicsSketch**—http://www.mainada.net/comics
- **Gnomz**—http://en.gnomz. com

Figure 3.11. Booktalking posting of C. Murdock's *Dairy Queen* using Blogger. Blogger copyright Google 2007.

Online Comic Creation Resources

Several online resources are available for students to use to create their own booktalk comics. These online tools will usually either allow a user to upload his/her own digital images or use available images and then add elements such as captions (see Figures 3.13 and 3.14). The following list of Web sites is a small representation of what is available:

- **Bubblr**—http://www.pim pampum.net/bubblr

- **Kerpoof**—http://www.kerpoof. com
- **MakeBeliefsComix.com** (see Figure 3.13)—http://www.makebeliefs comix.com
- **Patent Place Strip Creator**—http://www.patentplace.com
- **PikiStrips.com** (see Figure 3.14)—http://www.pikistrips.com
- **Quicktoons**—http://www.quick-toons.com
- **Read-Write-Think's Comic Creator**—http://www.readwrite think.org/materials/comic/index. html http://www.readwritethink. org/student_mat/student_materi al.asp?id=21
- **Scholastic Capt Underpants Comic creator**—http://www.scholastic. ca/captainunderpants/comic.htm

- **StripGenerator**—http://stripgenerator.com
- **Toondoo**—http://www.toondo.com

If Internet access is unavailable then consider obtaining a software program that can be used to create a cartoon.

Software

- **Comic Book Creator**—http://www.mycomic bookcreator.com
  - a program designed to create comics for print, Web, blog, or e-mail.
- **Hollywood High**—http://www.scholastic.com
  - scripting writing and cartoon production from Scholastic/Theatrix
- **Comic Life** (Mac)—http://plasq.com
  - Available as a free, 30-day trial from Plasq. Included in some Mac OS X versions.

Figure 3.12. *Captain Blood* cartoon booktalk. Copyright © Overdue Media LLC and used with permission.

WIKIS

A wiki is a collaborative Web site on which content can be quickly created or edited by anyone who has access to it. The name *wiki* comes from the Hawaiian word *wiki wiki*, which means quickly or rapidly. Wikis are about collaborative writing and are a wonderful tool for sharing booktalks.

There are several wiki hosting sites on the Internet that are free for educators. Three popular ones are:

Wikispaces: http://www.wikispaces.com
Pbwiki: http://pbwiki.com
Wetpaint: http://www.wetpaint.com

Figure 3.13. MakeBeliefsComix.com: An online tool that allows users to create a three-panel strip by selecting from available character pictures and then adding their own text.

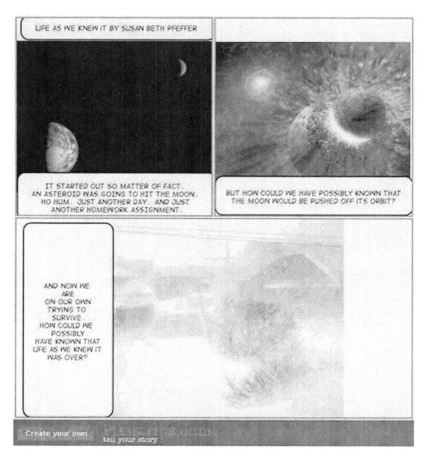

Figure 3.14. Cartoon booktalk on Pfeffer's *Life as We Knew It* created with uploaded images to the PikiStrips Web site (http://www.pikis trips.com/ps/gallery/view_image/14351132).

Figure 3.15. pbwiki site (http://pbwiki.com/) for collaborative writing.

Each of these sites offers free hosting for educators and offers security necessary for student use.

Pbwiki

To begin your booktalking wiki, you first need to sign up for a site to post your booktalks. This is a fairly standard process in each of the wiki hosting sites. Go to the pbwiki site (http://pbwiki.com/) to get started (see Figure 3.15).

As part of the sign-up process you will need to choose a name for your site. This can be your name, your school/library name, a class name, and so forth. Under **Tell us about your new wiki,** be sure to choose **For education** (see Figure 3.16). This will ensure your site will not contain advertising. If this option is not available, e-mail the wiki site to explain that you are using the wiki for education and ads will be removed from your page.

Once you have completed the account application you will be sent a confirmation e-mail message. You will need to access that e-mail message and click on the link to create your wiki. You will then be able to choose a password and decide whether your wiki will be public or private (see Figure 3.17). If you are building a class wiki, you may want to keep the wiki private.

Now that the options have been set for your wiki, you are ready to start creating your content. From your pbwiki front page you can begin editing the page content and adding new pages for different booktalks (see Figure 3.18).

Your front page should introduce the project and explain the purpose of your wiki (see Figure 3.19). To edit your site select the **Edit page** button. Writing in the wiki is done online using the Web browser. While editing, you should see familiar tools above the edit window, such as those used in a word processor.

Students can create their own wiki pages for their booktalks. On each booktalking page that students create, they should include bibliographical information for the book they are focusing on along with their written booktalk (see Figure 3.20).

Click on **Save,** and you now have a page created in your student wiki. Pages are easy to create and easy to edit.

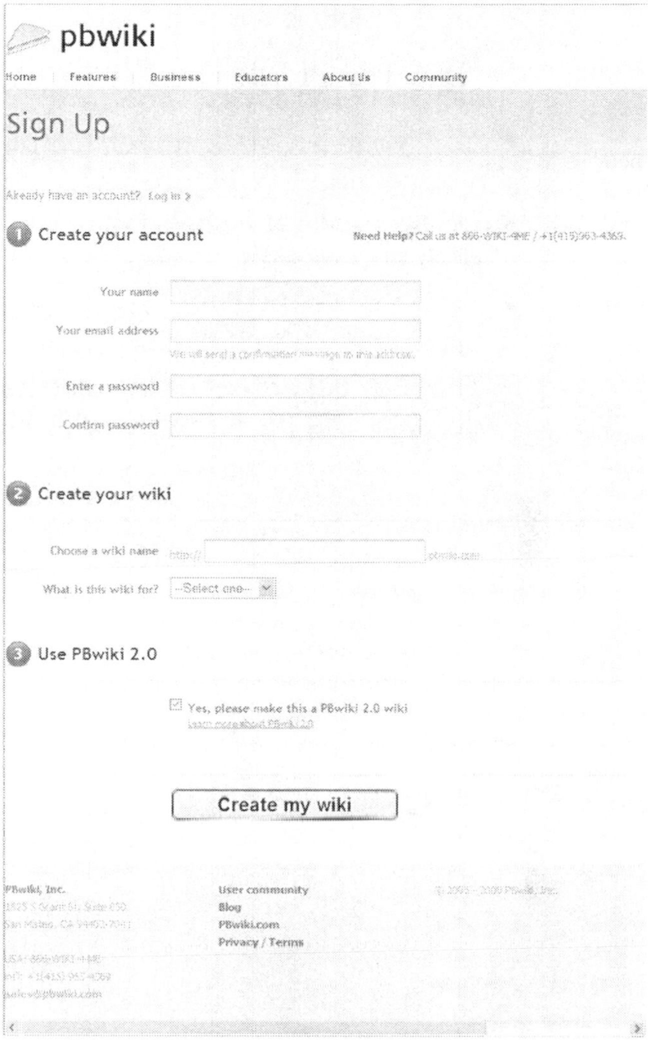

SHELF TALKERS

Let Your Shelves Do the Talking for You

No librarian, media specialist, or teacher can always be in the stacks or classroom collection to give booktalks. Why not have your shelves do the talking for you? Create your own "shelf talkers." All you need is Internet access, word processing software, and a printer—preferably a color printer.

To create a shelf talker, you will need an image of the book jacket and a short blurb describing the book. Use your booktalks or pull them from the Internet. The booktalks may need to be shortened to fit on the shelf talker. Then print the new shelf talker onto paper or card stock and place them on the shelf with the book being talked (see Figure 3.21).

To create a shelf talker:

- Open your word processor to a blank page.
- Format the page into two columns. Set the margins to narrow [0.5"].
- Approximately 5" down in the first column, insert a copy of the book cover. These images can be found on the Internet on a variety of pages.

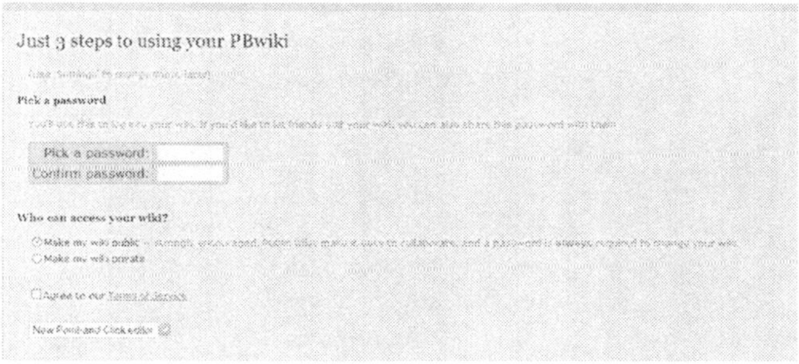

Figure 3.16. Creating a wiki account for educational uses at pbwiki.

Figure 3.17. Setting the password and collaboration levels for a pbwiki account.

- Set the picture wrap to "square."
- Type the call number, author, title, and publication information next to the picture of the cover.
- Add your booktalk under the publication information. Do the same in the next column (see Figure 3.22).
- Do not make the shelf talker too long because it will hide the books on the shelf underneath.
- Print the shelf talkers. This works better printed in color but can be done in black and white if that is all you have.
- The shelf talkers can be laminated or pasted onto card stock to make them more durable. Old file folders work well for this. If you have the capability, you can print them right onto card stock.
- Cut the page down the middle to separate the shelf talkers.
- Fold the shelf talker above the booktalk.
- Place them into the shelves. The top portion should be placed under the books to keep them in place.
- Have a supply of shelf talkers available to switch in and out as the books fly off the shelves.

Figure 3.18. Front page of a new wiki in pbwiki.

Figure 3.19. Booktalking wiki site being edited.

Figure 3.20. Sample booktalk being written into pbwiki.

Shelf talkers are a great student project. Have each student create his/her own shelf talker as a book project. These projects can be added to the library supply. If appropriate, have students sign their shelf talkers so that others know that the book is recommended by a student.

The book blurb is a short form of booktalking that is usually found on the back cover and would make a great shelf talker. For more instructions on how to write a book blurb, Marilynn Byerly has created a great resource. For example, Ms. Byerly suggests that when you are writing a book blurb about romantic suspense story, do the following:

First paragraph: Simple plot set up and main character's emotional involvement with it. What is the exterior conflict of the novel? (What are the hero and heroine fighting against and why?)

Second paragraph: More simple plot set up and hero's or second lead's emotional involvement with it.

Third and fourth paragraphs: What is the interior conflict of the novel? (What tears the hero and heroine apart emotionally?) What must both achieve or defeat, and what do they have to lose? This can include plot set up, place set up, the important secondary characters, and the villain (Byerly, 2005).

At her site titled *How to Write a Blurb*, Ms. Byerly has created paragraph by paragraph instructions on how she writes a book's back cover for a number of genres including romance, romantic suspense, mystery, science fiction, and fantasy (see Figure 3.23).

Figure 3.21. Shelf talker placed with the collection in the library. Book cover from *Life as We Knew It*, by Susan Beth Pfeffer. Copyright © 2006. Reprinted by permission of Houghton Mifflin Harcourt Publishing Company.

CREATING A BOOKMARK USING PUBLISHER2007

One way to use technology to advertise new books is to create bookmark booktalks for them. These bookmarks are easy to make, and students will be introduced to great books while using them.

There is no bookmark template in Publisher2007, but it is possible to create one that you can use. This procedure creates a sheet of bookmarks that are printed five per page on 8.5" x 11" paper, with room for trimming.

1. In the **Publication Types** list, click **Blank Page Sizes.**
2. Under **Standard**, click **Create custom page size**.
3. In the **Custom Page Size** dialog box, change **Layout Type** to Multiple pages per sheet. Type **2"** in the **Width** box, and then type **7.5"** in the **Height** box. In **Target sheet size,** choose **Custom.** Type 11" in **Sheet width,** 8.5" in **Sheet height, Side margin** to .5"
4. In the **Name** box, enter Bookmarks.
5. Click **OK** to close the **Custom Page Size** dialog box, and then click **Create** to create the bookmark.

Customize your bookmark publication by adding pictures, graphics, or text. You can also customize by selecting color schemes or font schemes.

If you want to print content on the back of your bookmark, create a two-sided bookmark by adding a new page to your publication. On the **Insert** menu, click **Page.**

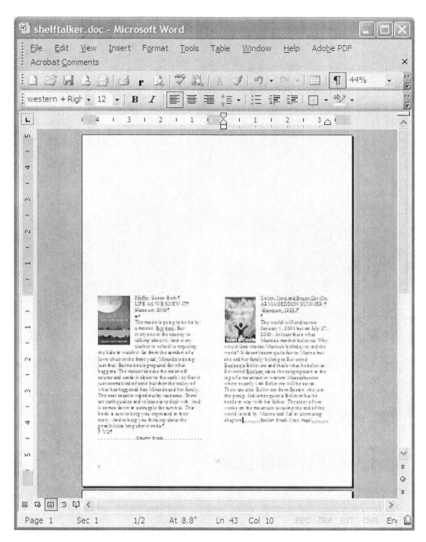

Figure 3.22. Creating a shelf talker using a word processor. Book cover from *Life as We Knew It*, by Susan Beth Pfeffer. Copyright © 2006. Reprinted by permission of Houghton Mifflin Harcourt Publishing Company.

6. To print your bookmark publication, click **Print** on the **File** menu, and then select the options that you want.

7. In the **Print** dialog box, under **Printing options**, select **Multiple copies per sheet**, and then click **Print**.

8. Under **More print options**, adjust the value in the **Side margin** box until you can see four bookmarks on the page under **Preview** (see Figure 3.24).

Notes

- If you are printing two-sided bookmarks on a duplex printer, you may need to change the options in the **Print** dialog box to choose how you want your publication to be printed on both sides of the paper. The available options in the **Print** dialog box vary, depending on your printer. If the **Two-sided, flip on short edge** option is available, select it to ensure that the content on each side of your bookmark is printed in the same direction. You should print a test sheet to determine what settings work best.

- If you are printing two-sided bookmarks to a nonduplex printer, you need to print the first side of your bookmark publication first and then flip the sheets, reinsert them into your printer feed tray, and then print the second side. Print a test sheet first to determine which direction you need to flip the paper before you print the second side.

- Print your bookmarks on heavy paper or card stock so that they are durable. Bookmarks can be printed on standard paper stock for short-term use.

BOOKTALK TRADING CARDS

One trick to use when you want to booktalk a group of books but don't have enough to go around is to create a set of booktalk trading cards. Students could create these cards as well. Students who are interested in a title being booktalked are given the trading cards. At the end of the booktalk session, students have a few minutes to trade their books. The student with the trading card can go to the library to exchange the card for the book.

It is easy to create trading cards using Word2007. Create a **blank presentation.** Choose **Page Layout** ribbon. In the **Page Setup** group, click the **Size** arrow. Choose **Index Card 3 x 5.** *Note: If you don't have Word2007 there is another Word format that works with earlier versions and uses a template described after this section.*

To create the cards, include a picture of the book cover on one side of the card. These cover images can be found on the Internet. The title and author of the book should be included on the front. The other side could include the Library of Congress summary note or a short booktalk (see Figure 3.25).

The trading cards can be printed on index cards or on standard paper. The paper can be glued onto the index cards for a heavier trading card. For longer life, laminate the cards before use.

Creating Booktalking Trading Cards Using Templates

Another way to create trading cards is to use a template, and print on 8.5" x 11" card stock or heavy bond paper.

Start the process by obtaining a digital image of the book cover to use on the front of the trading card.

Next, create your booktalking trading cards by downloading the trading card template from the DrsCavanaugh Web site (addresses below). This is

Figure 3.23. Screen capture from Marilynn Byerly's Web site (http://marilynnbyerly.com/marilynnbyerly/blurb.html) that explains how to write your own book blurb—a very short form of booktalking. Copyright © 2005 Marilynn Byerly.

Figure 3.24. Booktalking bookmarks created with MS Publisher. Book cover from *Life as We Knew It,* by Susan Beth Pfeffer. Copyright © 2006. Reprinted by permission of Houghton Mifflin Harcourt Publishing Company.

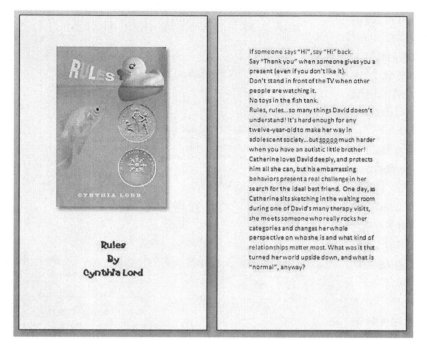

If someone says "Hi", say "Hi" back.
Say "Thank you" when someone gives you a present (even if you don't like it).
Don't stand in front of the TV when other people are watching it.
No toys in the fish tank.
Rules, rules...so many things David doesn't understand! It's hard enough for any twelve-year-old to make her way in adolescent society...but soooo much harder when you have an autistic little brother! Catherine loves David deeply, and protects him all she can, but his embarrassing behaviors present a real challenge in her search for the ideal best friend. One day, as Catherine sits sketching in the waiting room during one of David's many therapy visits, she meets someone who really rocks her categories and changes her whole perspective on who she is and what kind of relationships matter most. What was it that turned her world upside down, and what is "normal", anyway?

Figure 3.25. Booktalking trading card created with MS Word 2007. Cover from *Rules,* by Cynthia Lord. Copyright © 2006. Reprinted by permission of Scholastic. Rubber duck detail © Gary Doak/ Photonica. Goldfish detail © G.K. & Vikki Hart/Iconica.

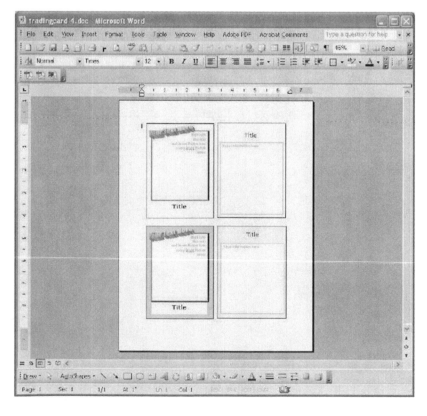

a very basic template, and you should feel free to add to it or make changes as you see fit. There are two different forms of the template available: one that makes two cards and the other that creates four cards (see Figure 3.26). Either click on the link and when prompted choose the **Save as** option, or right click on the link and save the template to your own computer.

The MS Word template for the trading card is available at:
http://www.drscavanaugh. org/digitalcamera/trading_ cards/tradingcard2.doc (2 cards)

http://www.drscavanaugh. org/digitalcamera/trading_ cards/tradingcard-4.doc (4 cards)

To add your book cover image to the trading cards, use the **insert** option from the word processor program. Highlight the indicated text and add your picture to the card where indicated by choosing the menu option **Insert,** then **Picture,** then **From file.** Browse to the desired picture location, select the picture, and click on **OK.** Adjust the size of your image to make it fit in the space on the card layout. First select the picture by clicking on it, then resize by pulling the corners to fit into the appropriate space. You may

Figure 3.26. Creating booktalking trading cards using a word processing two-card template.

wish to use your image tools to crop the image before or after adjusting the image size.

Now use the blank sections to title and write your booktalk. The report area is sufficient for one to two paragraphs (this will become the back of the card later). You can change the font size and style of the report section. Use the image as the focus of your writing. Be sure to add the book title and author to your card in the upper right and lower left sections. Now double click on the "Your Text Here" to create your own headline statement. Double clicking should open the Word Art pop-up window. Replace the highlighted statement with one of your own. You might want to use this area for the title and the bottom title section for the author's name.

Now print out the trading card using your printer. If you are using the four-card template, you will require two printings: once for the front and once for the back. After the card prints the first time, turn it over and print on the back of the paper. The template is designed so that the second printing should put a back on the image section and an image on the back section. Two-card templates will produce two identical cards. The four-card template will make identical sets at the top and bottom (although you can make these different).

Using your scissors, cut out the trading card. This sheet will create two identical trading cards, one to keep and one to share.

REFERENCES

American Association of School Librarians (AASL). (2007). AASL Standards for the 21st-Century Learner. Retrieved May 3, 2008, from http://www.ala.org/ala/aasl/aaslproftools/learningstandards/AASL_Learning_Standards_2007.pdf.

Bolter, J. D. (1991). *Writing Space: The Computer Hypertext, and the History of Writing.* New York: Erlbaum.

Byerly, Marilynn. (2005) "Writing the Back Cover Blurb." Retrieved August 24, 2007 from http://www.marilynnbyerly.com/marilynnbyerly/blurb.html.

Kamil, M. (2003). Adolescents and Literacy: Reading for the 21st Century. *Alliance for Excellent Education.* Retrieved April, 2005, from http://www.all4ed.org/publications/AdolescentsAndLiteracy.pdf.

Lenhart, A., Horrigan, J., & Fallows, D. (2004). Content Creation Online. *Pew Internet & American Life Project.* Retrieved July, 2005, from http://www.pewInternet.org/pdfs/PIP_Content_Creation_Report.pdf.

National School Boards Association. (2007). Creating & Connecting: Research and Guidelines on Online Social and Educational Networking. Retrieved August 21, 2007, from http://files.nsba.org/creatingandconnecting.pdf.

Wilhelm, Jeff. (2000, March). Literacy by Design: Why Is All This Technology So Important? *Voices from the Middle, 7*(3), 4.

4

Creating or Locating Images

IMAGES FOR YOUR BOOKTALK PRESENTATION

There are a number of ways to create images for booktalk presentations, depending on the tools and resources that are available.

Drawing Program

If you or your students like to draw with a computer you can use this method to create the images for your booktalk presentation. Make your picture with a program such as MS Paint, and then save your picture file to a folder on the computer for your booktalk.

1. Start your paint/drawing program, and use the tools available to create your images.
2. Once you have created the image, save the image to your project folder on the computer or in an attached storage device. From a drawing program it is usually best to save your picture as a GIF image.
3. Repeat the above procedure for each image you wish to use in your presentation.

Scanning

If you like to draw, or if students create their own images for their presentations using paint, colored pencils, or crayons, then scanning is a great way to digitize the pictures for their video booktalks. As a suggestion, you or your students might use the scanner software or your imaging software, such as Paint or Photoshop, to capture and edit images.

1. Place the first picture you want to use in your presentation onto the scanner.
2. Start your imaging program and look for an option (usually in the **File** menu) such as the **From Scanner or Camera...** or **Import** (see Figure 4.1). Depending on your software you may have to select the scanner from a set of options. A pop-up window will give you scanning options. Choose your scanner, click **OK,** and then a scanner window should appear.
3. Most scanner programs have both a **Scan** and a **Preview** option. Click the **Preview** option to make sure that the picture is correct, right side up, and lined up straight.

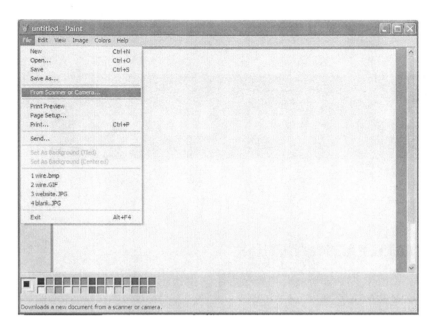

Figure 4.1. Adding a scanned image to the MS Paint program.

4. Depending on the program there may also be options for setting the resolution. Often the default is 300 dpi (dots per inch), which is fine for printing. But computer screens usually display at 75 dpi, so you should decrease the resolution. This change will also reduce the file size of the image. Now click the **Scan** button. Your image should be scanned and the picture placed into your picture program (see Figure 4.2).

5. Now save the scanned picture into your project's folder so that you can place it into your presentation later. It is suggested that you save your images as either JPEGs, GIFs, or PNGs as these should be understood by most programs: JPEGs are usually used with photographs, GIFs with drawings, and PNGs can be used with either.

6. Repeat the above procedure for each image you wish to use in your presentation.

Digital Camera

Another option is to use a digital camera and take your own photographs for your booktalk presentation. Use your digital camera to take pictures of artwork, live events, tableaus, or visuals desired for your booktalk presentation.

1. Most digital cameras connect to the computer through a USB port, and if the computer doesn't detect your camera as a camera, it will instead identify the camera as an additional drive (e.g., H). Plug one end of its cable to the camera and the other into one of the computer's USB ports.

2. First you will need to select the pictures in the camera that you wish to use for your project. These images will be moved or copied to your project folder. Open the camera's drive folder that has the pictures inside. To do this you may need to go through My Computer, choose the camera from the desktop, or select open as a folder.

3. Next open your project folder.

4. Now drag the images that you want to use from the camera's folder to your project folder. Most cameras today store their pictures as JPEG images, which usually work well for creating the booktalks.

5. Repeat the above procedure for each image you wish to use in your presentation.

Internet

You can download pictures from the Internet for your projects. For example, using the Google search engine, you can search for pictures on any subject and then save them to your hard drive to be inserted into your booktalk project folder. There are also a number of sites that provide copyright-free clipart and photographs. Make sure that you are allowed to use a picture that you find on the Web. To save a picture from the Web to your project folder:

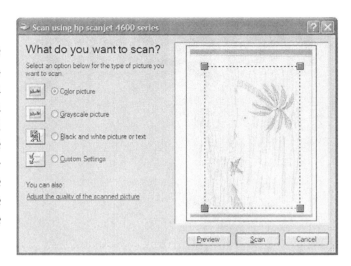

Figure 4.2. Using a scanner to capture a drawing.

1. Locate the image you would like to download.
2. Click on the image using the mouse button.

   PC/Windows—right click on the image and from the popup menu select the menu option that allows you to save the image
   MAC—hold the mouse button down for few seconds on the picture and from the popup menu select the menu option that allows you to save the image

3. Save the image to your computer by browsing to your project folder and then clicking on **OK**.

Sources for Shared or Public Domain Images

Note: Some of these sites offer images made accessible by the general public, which may not be appropriate for student or classroom use. As with any Internet resource, teachers should check to make sure that the site's images are appropriate and comply with your school and district guidelines.

- **Classroom Clipart:** http://classroomclipart.com
- **CopyrightFreePhotos.com:** http://www.copyrightfreephotos.com/default.aspx
- **Flickr:** http://www.flickr.com
- **FreeFoto.com:** http://www.freefoto.com/index.jsp
- **Gimp-Savvy:** http://gimp-savvy.com/PHOTO-ARCHIVE
- **Library of Congress—Prints and Photos:** http://www.loc.gov/rr/print/catalog.html
- **Morguefile.com:** public domain images for educational use, http://www.morguefile.com
- **NASA:** http://www.nasa.gov
- **NOAA:** http://www.photolib.noaa.gov/collections.html

Figure 4.3. MorgueFile is a digital photo-sharing Web site that provides quality images (http://www. morguefile.com/).

- **Open Clipart Library:** http://www. openclipart.org
- **Open Photo:** http://openphoto.net (see Figure 4.3)
- **Pics4Learning:** http://pics.tech4 learning.com

Using Your Pictures

To use the pictures you collect in your project folder, you will need to follow the directions for the software you are using to add pictures. Most programs use similar processes such as having an **Insert** menu item that can **insert Picture**. Often you choose the **From File...** option and browse to your project folder. Once you find the picture that you want, click once on it, and press the **Insert** button.

STORYBOARDS

A successful booktalk begins with good planning. Spending some time organizing ideas and gathering material, such as the images you will use, will save time and effort in the long run and make your booktalk presentation more organized and meaningful to your viewers. Storyboarding is a design and management tool that assists the thinking process and provides a visual outline of a project with its associated text.

In *ARTiculating: Teaching Writing in a Visual World*, Eric H. Hobson suggests storyboarding as a prewriting activity where students quickly and roughly sketch pictures with the basics of a narrative (Childers, Hobson, & Mullin, 1998). In the case of a technology-enhanced booktalk, storyboarding may not be the prewriting activity, but it could be used as the writing activity in a multimedia project where students make rough drawings of the kinds of pictures that they will use and the basics for their narration. This kind of writing activity can help visual thinkers compose their topic overview and begin the structure of their narrative. Some of the

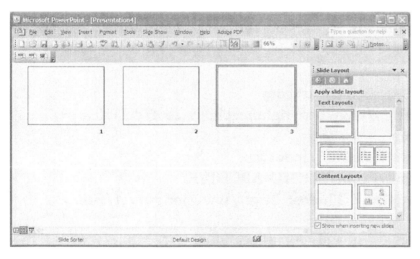

Figure 4.4. Using the slide sorter to create storyboards with PowerPoint.

advantages of using a storyboard in multimedia development include:

- a common document that can be used by a cooperative group as a point of reference;
- a tool to focus on content; and
- a tool to identify missing components or needs.

For the classroom, storyboarding can also be used as a writing or planning assessment. Storyboards can be completed as homework or designed together in classroom cooperative groups. Additionally, creating the storyboard is an activity that students can do during their nontech time, such as before going to the computer lab or when other students or groups are using the computer in the classroom.

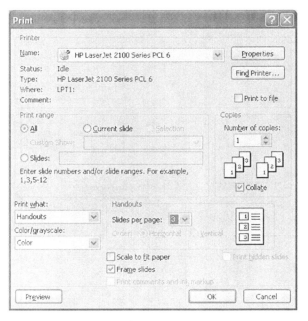

Figure 4.5. Setting the print options to create a storyboard with PowerPoint.

Creating Blank Storyboards

The following three methods can be used to create blank storyboards: online using an online service, using PowerPoint, and using a word processing program.

Creating Storyboards from PDF Pad

PDF Pad (http://www.pdfpad.com/storyboards) is a comprehensive online service with which users can select, create, download, and print high-quality templates for projects, free of charge or registration hassles. Along with various forms of

Student Instructions for Writing a Storyboard

Create a storyboard to help you organize your thoughts/ideas/content for your booktalk. First decide on the kind of booktalk that you are going to give, then pick a number, such as five, and then determine the five most important things to include about your booktalk. For example, if you were going to do a plot booktalk, decide on the five things necessary to understand the story (but don't tell the ending), and use those five for your storyboard. As you do your storyboards, look to see if you need to add more information to make your booktalk more understandable.

1. In your presentation, you should always include the title, author, and genre for the book you will booktalk about.
2. As you complete your storyboard, each section represents a visual slide of the presentation.
3. Number or label each section with just a few words that represent the title of the slide.
4. In the box, draw a rough sketch or describe the kind of picture you would like to use.
5. Next to the drawing, create an outline of what you will talk about or script your narration.
6. Repeat the process for each slide.

Remember that if the order is not to your liking, you can rearrange the sequence later.

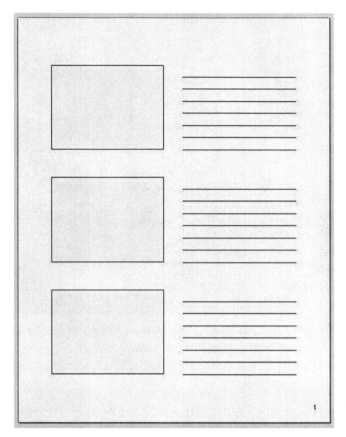

Figure 4.6. Sample blank storyboard created with PowerPoint.

Figure 4.7. Inserting a table into MS Word for storyboarding.

graph paper, the site also will create downloadable PDF-formatted storyboards on demand. The storyboards are available in various aspect ratios including Square (1:1), television (4:3) or wide screen (16:9). Each of the different aspect ratios also creates storyboards with differing numbers of scenes. Square has spaces for 12 scenes, television for 9 scenes, and wide screen for 6 scenes.

To print your storyboards from PDF Pad:

1. Go the Web site at http://www.pdfpad.com/storyboards.
2. *Choose cell ratio* for the size preferred for the storyboard (Square, Television, Widescreen).
3. *Choose the paper* size from the dropdown list.
4. Click on the *Print* button.
5. When the PDF of the storyboard shows, print the number of pages desired.

Creating Storyboards from PowerPoint

To create a storyboard for your booktalk, start PowerPoint, then select **File**, then **New**. Now from the New Presentation menu choose the Blank Presentation option with the basic design. Using the title slide for the rest of the storyboard design is fine.

To create your storyboard sheet you will need three blank slides. The easy way to do this is to change to the **Slide Sorter** display from the **View** menu, and then copy the first blank page, and then paste it two more times. To copy the blank page click on it once then choose **Copy** from the **Edit** menu. Next select **Paste** from the **Edit** menu (see Figure 4.4). *A quick way to add the blank pages is to press the control and V keys at the same time to paste, or control and D to duplicate.*

Printing the Storyboard. Now print your blank "presentation" as a "**Notes**" version of the PowerPoint. Select Print from the File menu. From the pop-up window change the "**Print what**" dropdown to Handouts, and in the Handouts options change the "**Slides per page:**" dropdown to 3, this way you get the blank lines for noting or story writing. Now press the **OK** button, and print out your storyboard handouts, and get started writing your story (see Figure 4.5).

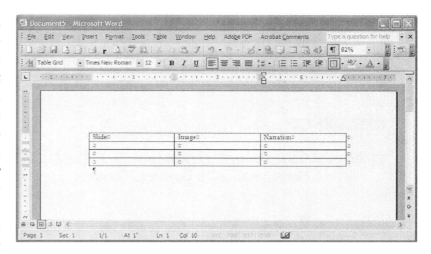

Figure 4.8. Adding titles to the table for the storyboard.

As you write your storyboard, make rough sketches in the blank slide section to show the way you want your slides to look. You can either find or create the final pictures later. In the lined section, write out either the script or an outline of the narration for the booktalk (see Figure 4.6).

Creating Storyboards from a Word Processor

Using the word processor, choose the option to create a table. In MS Word this can be done either though the table button or by selecting menu item **Table**, then **Insert**, then **Table**...

Create a table that is three columns wide and at least 4 rows tall (see Figure 4.7).

Next add titles to the first row in each cell to create the elements of the storyboard: Slide, Image, Narration (see Figure 4.8).

Adjust the width of the first column to be just a bit wider than the title. Then adjust the other two column widths so that they fill up the rest of the page width. In the space under the narration title, add underlines to create space for text, creating at least 5 to 10 blank lines. Do this for the other two boxes

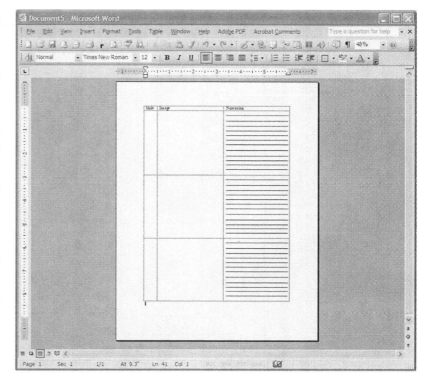

Figure 4.9. Completed storyboard sheet using MS Word.

under the narration column. Add enough lines so that the table fills the page but doesn't continue onto a second page (see Figure 4.9). Then print sheets for the students to use in designing their projects. It is a good idea to print extra sheets in case students make errors or want to do even more.

REFERENCE

Childers, P. B., Hobson, E. H., & Mullin, J. A. (1998). *ARTiculating: Teaching Writing in a Visual World.* Portsmouth, NH: Boynton/Cook.

5

Presentation Booktalks

Text-based booktalks using technology add a new dimension to booktalking. We are now ready to take it up another notch by adding presentation software to the booktalk.

IN THE CLASSROOM

Vox Middle School has approximately 1,200 students and is located in a residential neighborhood. At each grade level students are divided into three teams or houses of about 150 students each. In one of the eighth-grade teams, the Hawk team, English teacher Jennifer Ross, science teacher Freddie Baldur, and school media specialist Kesia Livingston work together on an interdisciplinary unit during the third nine weeks that uses the novel *Flush* by Carl Hiaasen as its focus. In the *Flush* unit, students are achieving a number of language arts standards for reading and writing along with science standards for ecosystems, interrelationships, and interactions. Adding a booktalk component will also address AASL standards. While reading the book the students work on reading activities in their English class including directed reading and journaling. In their science class the students are learning science content associated with the reading though lectures, activities, and labs. In the library research book collections on related topics are set up along with other book collections from the same genre. Ms. Livingston also works with individual students and small groups on their projects. Library resources are also structured for use by students in creating their multimedia projects. At the end of the unit the students in the Hawk team will be rotated though the library to take the Accelerated Reader test for the *Flush* novel. As the culminating activity of the book, students work with the library media specialist in cooperative groups on a multimedia project that is presented to the class. As part of their differentiated instruction plan, Ms. Livingston, Ms. Ross, and Mr. Baldur instruct the students to choose their projects based on their own interests. Then the teachers use the student choices to assemble class groups for their projects. The projects choices include:

- *Inference Advertisements:* analysis of magazine/online advertisements concerning gambling along with the creation of a PSA magazine ad for the environment.
- *Science Inquiry Project:* simulating a pollutant plume tracing in a local water resource and reporting the results.

- *Persuasive Writing Assignment:* the writers must convince readers to take action or to change their opinions about the environment or gambling.
- *Electronic Booktalk Presentations:* using PowerPoint or other presentation software about the book *Flush* and another associated book selected from a list of available texts in the library.

Lesson Plan for Electronic Booktalk Presentations

Purpose/Outcomes/Objectives:

The purpose of this lesson is to practice public speaking and presentations. Students will create an electronic form of presentation as a booktalk. The overall goal of the booktalk is to persuade the audience to read the book. The final projects will be posted for the entire class to share.

- Students will create a booktalk using a presentation program.
- Students will share/present their booktalk projects using the presentation tool.

Standards

AASL

1.2.3 Demonstrate creativity by using multiple resources and formats.

2.1.4 Use technology and other information tools to analyze and organize information.

3.2.3 Demonstrate teamwork by working productively with others.

4.3.1 Participate in the social exchange of ideas, both electronically and in person. (AASL, 2007)

Language Arts (example Florida Language Arts Standards):

Writing:

- LA.8.3.1.1—generating ideas from multiple sources based upon teacher-directed topics and personal interests;
- LA.8.3.1.2—making a plan for writing that addresses purpose, audience, main idea, logical sequence, and time frame for completion;
- LA.8.3.5.1—prepare writing using technology in a format appropriate to audience;
- LA.8.3.5.3—share the writing with the intended audience.

Media Literacy:

- LA.8.6.3.2—demonstrate the ability to select and ethically use print and non-print media appropriate for the purpose, occasion, and audience to develop into a formal presentation.

Technology:

- LA.8.6.4.1—use appropriate available technologies to enhance communication and achieve a purpose (e.g., video, digital technology); and
- LA.8.6.4.2—evaluate and apply digital tools to publications and presentations.

INSTRUCTIONS

One of the best ways to learn about good books is through word of mouth. When we hear our friends talking about a book they really liked, we are more apt to pick it up to read it than we are if it's on a suggested reading list!

During this quarter, you have all read at least one book of your own choosing. Now you are going to share a book with your classmates. For this assignment, you will deliver a booktalk on your book using presentation software, such as PowerPoint. In preparing your booktalk PowerPoint presentation you should use visuals, sounds, and text to convey the feeling of the book. Your PowerPoint presentation should complement your oral presentation but should also be able to stand on its own. The PowerPoint presentations will be published on the school Web site though the library page.

What Is a Booktalk?

I like to use the analogy of a movie trailer. The purpose of a booktalk is to "sell" the book. You want to give enough of the plot to interest the listeners, but you are not giving only a summary of the book. You don't want to give away the important parts of the book. You certainly never want to give away the ending. You want to highlight the interesting points. You may want to read certain passages to your listeners. The main purpose of a booktalk is to grab the audience's interest and make them want to read the book. It's always a good idea to end the booktalk with a cliffhanger. Booktalks are usually presented to groups of students. The booktalker presents the booktalks orally and should use the book as a visual prop. For tips on how to present a booktalk, see Nancy Keane's Booktalking Tips at http://www.nancykeane.com/booktalks/tips.htm. When assessing the final project, you may want to provide separate rubrics for the booktalk (Table 5.1) and the PowerPoint (Table 5.2).

Rubric for Booktalk

Table 5.1
Rubric for Booktalk

	1	2	3
Has book in hand			
Includes title, author, and publication information			
Uses an introduction that grabs the audience's attention			
Maintains eye contact			
Uses information from the book (e.g. names of characters and places)			
Demonstrates enthusiasm for book			
Uses interesting passages from book			
Tells enough to gain interest but does not reveal the ending of the book			
Uses conclusion that makes us want to read the book			
Stays within time limits			
Overall presentation			
Comments:			

Rubric for PowerPoint Presentation

Table 5.2
Rubric for PowerPoint Presentation

	1	2	3
Minimum of 10 slides			
Title, author, and publication information for the book			
Graphics convey the feeling of the book			
Cover of the book			
Spelling and grammar			
Can stand on its own without oral presentation			
Conveys the sense of the book			
Overall presentation			
Comments			

POWERPOINT XP

Perhaps the most commonly used presentation software is PowerPoint. Presentation tools such as Microsoft's PowerPoint or other presentation applications can be used to create presentation booktalks, and you can even add your own voice narration to the presentation. These booktalks can be "played" on a computer or presented in person. By using a video projector or large screen television connected to a computer, an instructor can present the booktalk to the whole class to use as an instructional reading activity, or to use the booktalk as an example. These digitally created booktalks have the added advantage that they can be saved onto a CD or online and made available at the students' home for outside viewing.

The easiest way to start creating your presentation booktalk is to create a folder on the computer or on an attached storage drive in which to store all your files, and then you can create or choose a template to use for your presentation. A large number of templates and themes are available that you can use to start your PowerPoint Booktalk. Using a template (whether you download it or create your own) saves you time, makes the presentation look appealing, and ensures that the text is readable.

Create a folder on the computer for your presentation booktalk so that you have all the necessary files in a common location and you won't have to look for them. For example, if you burn your booktalk to a CD you will also need to make sure that any sound or video files are transferred to the CD also. If you don't have PowerPoint try downloading and using Open Office's presentation tool (discussed later in this chapter).

Creating the Booktalk

To start your new booktalk in PowerPoint select **File**, then **New**. Now from the *New Presentation* menu choose the *General Templates* button and then from the *General* tab choose a design (see Figure 5.1). You are now ready to start creating your booktalk.

To start your booktalk you will need a number of blank pages or slides, and you will most likely first need to create a storyboard for your booktalk (see Chapter 4 for more information on storyboards).

Adding text to your booktalk slides is not much different from using a regular word processor. On each page there should be a placeholder with the statement "Click to add text," so you'll do just that (see Figure 5.2). Click in the box and write elements of your

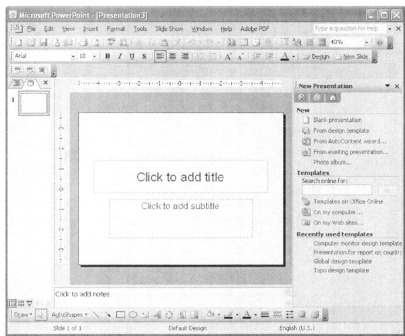

Figure 5.1. Starting a presentation in PowerPoint.

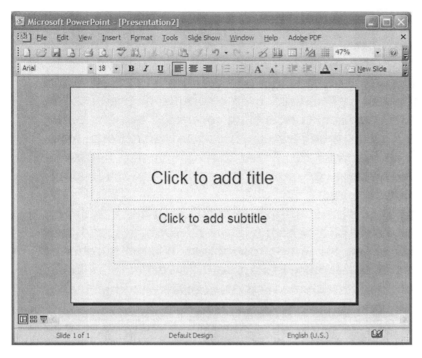

Figure 5.2. Adding text to the presentation.

presentation. Items such as the title, author, characters, and so forth make up your story. If you need to, you can reposition the text boxes or add a new text box using the drawing tools or from the **Insert** menu.

When you add your text the program may automatically resize some of it to fit within the text box. You can leave it this way or resize it yourself using either the adjust text size tools on the tool bar or by formatting the font size (**Format—Font**).

Images

Now it's time to add some pictures to your booktalk. Pictures can come from a wide variety of sources, such as digital cameras, scanned drawings, computer drawing programs, and even from on-line sources of clipart and photographs (see Chapter 4). You can even mix the sources up a bit, such as by using an image from the Internet, and then manipulating that image with software to remove parts, change parts, or turn it into a different kind of picture. With some image programs you can take a photograph image and turn it into a charcoal drawing.

To add an image to your slide:

1. View to the slide where you want to add the picture;
2. From the **Insert** menu, select **Picture.** Depending on the type of picture you are adding, you can choose **Clipart, From file...,** or **From Scanner or Camera** (see Figure 5.3).
3. From your menu selection, such as **From File...,** you will need to browse through the available options and

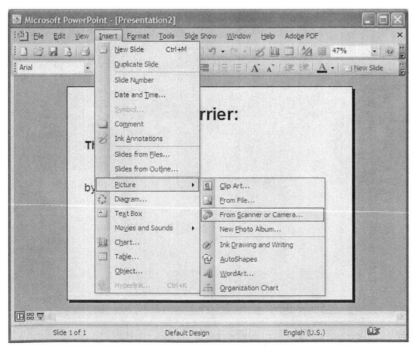

Figure 5.3. Inserting an image into the presentation.

select the image that you want, then click the **Insert** button.

4. Your picture should now be added to the slide.
5. Repeat this process for each slide page where you want to add images.

Narration

With just a microphone plugged into your computer's sound card, you can add narration to your booktalk presentation. Before you go further you need to make sure that PowerPoint will embed the narration sound files and save them with the booktalk presentation file.

To make sure that all your narration sound is saved:

1. Click on the **Tools** menu and choose **Options;**
2. Now choose the *General* tab and change the *Link sounds with files size greater than* to 50,000 Kb, which is the highest it will go, and;
3. Then click the **OK** button.

To add your narration to a slide of your booktalk:

1. View that slide or page and then select the **Insert** menu;
2. Select the **Movies and Sounds** option, and then choose the **Record Sound** option (see Figure 5.4).
3. A pop-up window will appear that you can use to record your voice.
4. Click on the red circle to start recording and click on the square to stop. Click on the button with the triangle to playback your recording. Change the name of the *Record Sound* file to the page or slide number/title in the booktalk and then click the OK button. A speaker symbol will now appear on the page.
5. Once you have the speaker symbol on the page you can set the sound so that it will play by itself by using the **Custom Animation** option in the **Slide Show** menu.
6. A sidebar will show for *Custom Animation.* Use the dropdown menu next to the *Media* item, and select the option for the narration to "Start After Previous."

Repeat this process for the rest of your booktalk, adding

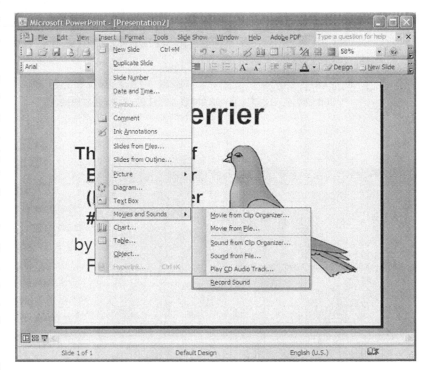

Figure 5.4. Adding narration to a slide in a presentation.

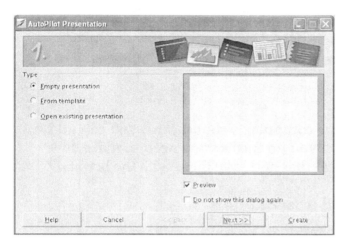

Figure 5.5. Creating a presentation using Open Office.

images, narration, and then setting the narration to run automatically.

USING POWERPOINT AS A BOOKTALK SCREENSAVER

Another use of PowerPoint is to post a booktalk screensaver. This is an especially good way to showcase student booktalks.

The first step is to create a booktalk in PowerPoint

Directions for making a PowerPoint screensaver with a Windows computer:

- Open your PowerPoint presentation.
- Choose **File,** then **Save As.**
- In the "Save as type:" dropdown list box, choose GIF, JPEG or PNG.
- Browse to your **My Pictures** folder (it's inside My Documents).
- Type in a file name and click **Save.**
- When PowerPoint asks if you want to export every slide in the presentation, click **Yes.** When the export completes, you'll have one image file for each slide in your presentation in your My Pictures folder.
- Now quit PowerPoint.
- Right click the Windows desktop and choose **Properties.**
- Click the *Screen Saver* tab.
- In the dropdown listbox under "Screen Saver" choose "My Pictures Slideshow."
- Click Settings if you want to fine-tune the results, such as for how long each image will show.
- Your PowerPoint is now your screensaver. Note that animation, transition, sounds, and narration will not be present.

BOOKTALKS WITH OPEN OFFICE PRESENTATION

Open Office (or Star Office) is a free productivity suite of tools. This open source program suite includes applications such as a word processor, a drawing program, a spreadsheet, and a presentation program. Versions of Open Office are available for the Macintosh, Windows, and Linux platforms. Open Office's presentation program, Impress, has the ability not only to

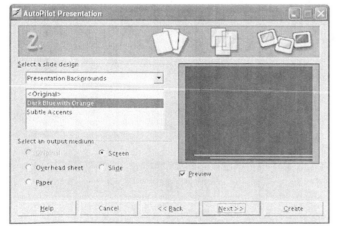

Figure 5.6. Selecting the slide design in Open Office.

save a presentation in its own format (.sxi), but also as a PowerPoint, which can then be played with any program that can play PowerPoint files (.ppt, .pps), or as a Flash file, which can be played using an Internet browser. One drawback of the Open Office option is that the narration for the book-talk must be done by recording each slide's audio track using another program, such as Sound Recorder or Audacity, and then inserting that audio into the slide.

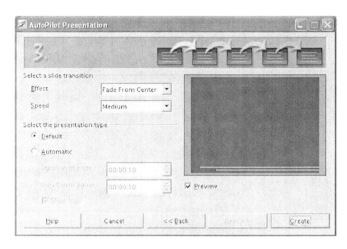

Figure 5.7. Choosing the slide transitions.

Open Office Software: http://www. opensoffice.org

Recording iLecture: http://www.lib. uiowa.edu/commons/ilecture

If you don't already have Open Office you will need to download the correct version for your computer's platform and install the software.

1. After the Open Office Suite has been installed, start the Impress presentation program.
2. When the program launches, you will first go through a simple three-step process to get started. The first step is to determine if you wish to create a new presentation, use a template, or open an existing presentation. If you are creating a new booktalk, select the option for an **Empty presentation** and then click on **Next** (see Figure 5.5).
3. Next you will determine what kind of design you are using. Here you can choose from backgrounds for your presentation. For your booktalk make sure that the medium chosen is the **Screen,** and then click on **Next** (see Figure 5.6).
4. The third step is to preset the slide transitions (although this can also be changed later). Decide if you want a special effect with the slide transitions (changing from one slide to the next) and how fast you want it to change. Also you can set the presentation type to either **Default,** which means advancing by clicking, or **Automatic,** where

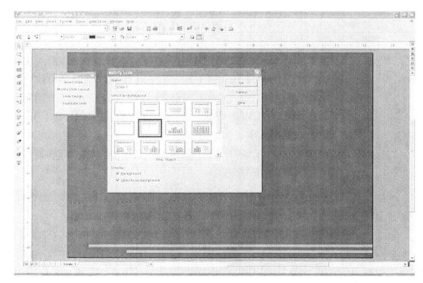

Figure 5.8. Choosing slide types for presentation.

the slide is displayed for a specific number of seconds. For right now, set the presentation type to **Default** if you are giving your booktalk in person or if you are planning a self-presenting booktalk, and then click on **Create** (see Figure 5.7).

5. The program next displays the working view for creating your presentation and will present you with the options for the type of slide design you can use (see Figure 5.8).

6. From this point on, the program is very similar to other presentation programs, such as MS PowerPoint, in creating the presentation slides. With each slide of the booktalk you can include images, text, and more (such as Web links).

7. Users can add an image onto a slide either by copying and pasting the image, such as from the Web, or by inserting an image as a file that has been saved on a drive. The program can use images in most of the common image formats.

To add a saved image to the presentation

Select the slide on which you want to place the image.
Click on **Insert** from the menu bar, then **Picture,** then **From file...**
A dialog box will open to allow the user to browse to the image file.
Once the image file is selected, click on the Open button to insert the image into the presentation.

Audio Narration

Currently, the Open Office program does not support narration, but it can include audio files. To add your own audio narration to the presentation you will need to create the audio for each slide using another program, such as Recorder or Audacity (see Chapters 6 and 7 for information on recording audio). Save each slide's narration as a separate file, and then insert that file into the presentation.

To add audio narration to the presentation

Select the slide on which you want to place the audio.
Click on **Insert** from the menu bar, then **Movie and Sound,** then **From file...**
A dialog box will open to allow the user to browse to the audio file.
Once the image file is selected, click on **Open** to insert the sound into the presentation.
A sound icon will appear on the slide. Resize the icon to make it less intrusive to your presentation.

When setting the length of time to display the slide, make sure that the slide's timing is set for longer than the audio narration.

Another option for adding narration to slides is to use a program such as iLecture (http://www.lib.uiowa.edu/commons/ilecture). However, using this program will create a final file that can be played with a browser but not with the presentation software.

FLASH VIDEO BOOKTALK

Flash was developed by Macromedia to allow people to create objects such as animations, presentations, and interactive objects. There are several products available that allow users to create flash objects without learning the flash programming language. Products such as Flash Slideshow Maker can be used to edit and organize your digital pictures, add transitions and sound, and then save the finished presentation as flash video. Flash video (.swf) has become a very common format and is used in sites such as YouTube, Google Video, and MySpace. Flash video can be played

Figure 5.9. Wizard window for Flash Slideshow Maker. Copyright © Anvsoft Inc. 2007.

on most computer operating systems using player programs such as QuickTime and Windows Media Player or played using a Web browser with the proper plug ins.

First, understand that you will not need to learn the flash programming language to create a flash booktalk. In this section, we describe how you can use the Flash Slideshow Maker program (http://www.flash-slideshow-maker.com) from ANVSoft Inc. to create a flash video booktalk on a computer running Windows. Using this program, a student, teacher, or library media specialist can begin with a collection of digital images and convert them into a flash video file format, which can be shown on a local computer or placed on the school or library Web site. The program also allows the user to add a soundtrack to the image collection in the form of music with the booktalk written on the slides or in the form of a narration using another audio program and importing the audio file as the soundtrack. While this program does not allow you to match up your audio narration with specific images, it can be a great addition to a booktalk created as an audio project such as a podcast. Then, using the podcast, the users can add images for the spoken booktalk.

If you don't already have it you will need to download and install Flash Slideshow Maker from the Web site (http://www.flash-slideshow-maker.com). After you have installed the software, start the Flash Slideshow Maker program and select the option to create a new project. Create your booktalk video using the program's three-step process after you have created the audio portion of the video.

Step 1: Creating the Narration

Begin the process by creating the narration for your booktalk. To do this you

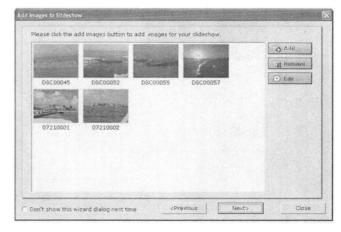

Figure 5.10. Browsing for images window for Flash Slideshow Maker. Copyright © Anvsoft Inc. 2007.

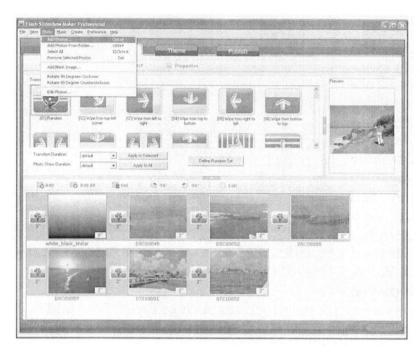

Figure 5.11. Selecting transitions for the presentation with Flash Slideshow Maker. Copyright © Anvsoft Inc. 2007.

will need to use another program, such as Audacity, to record the audio. See Chapter 6 for information and instructions for creating audio narrations. When you have finished recording the audio, save the file as an mp3, WMA, or WAV file; these formats can be imported into the Flash Slideshow Maker program.

Step 2: Import and Arrange Your Pictures

When you start the Flash Slideshow Maker program, a support wizard will display to help get you started (see Figure 5.9). Click on the **Next]** button to start the process of adding images to your presentation. If you don't want to use the wizard, click on the close button.

Next select the images that you will want to use from your computer, a disc, or a key drive. If you selected the **Next]** button then press on the **+Add** button to browse on your computer to where your images are stored. If you are not using the wizard, click on the **Photo** menu and then **Add Photos** to begin browsing for your images (see Figure 5.10). Once all the desired images are selected, then select the **Open** button to add them to your presentation. It is also suggested that this is a good time to leave the wizard to make some specific adjustments, in which case click on the **Close** button.

In the main Flash Slideshow Maker program, under the **Photo** tab, click on the **Transition Effect** tab. Here you can arrange the images by clicking and dragging the images into the order desired in the storyboard section at the bottom of the window (see Figure 5.11). You can also set the amount of time for the transitions between images and how long an individual image will show. To change the timing for any transition or image, first click on the image, choose the time from the drop-down, and then click on

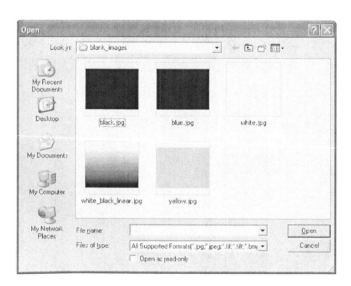

Figure 5.12. Creating blank slides for titles or credits with Flash Slideshow Maker. Copyright © Anvsoft Inc. 2007.

either the **Apply to Selected** or **Apply to All** button. Each picture and transition can have a different display time.

The program provides over 60 different transition effects that can be used as one picture changes to another. To set a transition effect, either drag the thumbnail from the **Transition Effects** area into the space between the images, click on the transition icon between the images, and then double click on the transition effect desired; or right-click on the transition icon between the images, select **Transition,** then select the transition by name from the list.

The software can also add blank images, such as for creating titles. Add blank images by clicking on the **Photo** menu and select **Add Blank Image...** This will cause a new pop-up window that can be used to select from five different blank images (see Figure 5.12). Alternatively, students or instructors could make additional blank im-

Figure 5.13. Adding text to an image in a presentation with Flash Slideshow Maker. Copyright © Anvsoft Inc. 2007.

ages with another program and then save them into the project folder for later use.

Clicking on the **Edit** button or double clicking on one of the images will produce a pop-up window for making additions to the image (see Figure 5.13). There are three kinds of edits that can be done. Under the **Info** tab the user can give the picture a title, and if there is an associated Web resource the URL can be added. Under the **Text** tab, users can select a font and add text to a picture, such as the name of a character or the story location. The text box added to the image can be repositioned by clicking and dragging. Double clicking in the text box will allow it to be edited. The **ArtClip** tab allows the user to add art onto the selected image, such as for adding a speech bubble or frame onto the image.

Step 3: Choosing a Display Theme

The Flash Slideshow Maker program can also display a theme for the presentation. These themes are templates that determine the look of the finished presentation, such as the addition of a frame around the main image, or how thumbnails of the

Figure 5.14. Choosing a theme and adding sound to the booktalk presentation with Flash Slideshow Maker. Copyright © Anvsoft Inc. 2007.

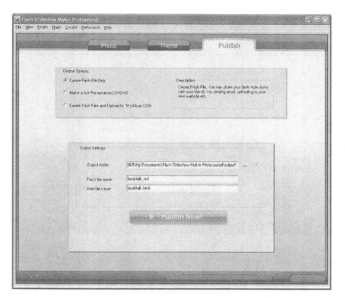

Figure 5.15. Finishing the presentation by saving it as a Flash Video with Flash Slideshow Maker. Copyright © Anvsoft Inc. 2007.

image presentation will be shown. Click on the **Theme** tab to choose from the available themes (see Figure 5.14). To select from the over 50 possible themes for your presentation use the slider bar to see the available options. Clicking on the desired theme will cause it to be highlighted and selected. This choice is not locked. Click on another theme to select it instead. In the theme section there is an option to provide a name for the presentation. A good idea is to write the book's name and author in the **Album Title** box. In many of the themes the text written in the **Album Title** box will appear at the top of the presentation.

Here the user can add the narration or music for the presentation. The soundtrack for the presentation can be created with another program, such as Audacity (see chapter 6 for making audio booktalks) or can come from a source such as an audio CD. The program can use audio files in mp3, WMA, or WAV formats. To add a recorded narration, click on the **Add** button in the **Background Music for Slide Show** section, browse to the desired music, and click on the **Open** button. The program will not automatically adjust the presentation time to the audio file, so it may be necessary to go back to the Photo section and adjust the display time of the images or add more pictures to the presentation. This adjustment is important if the added sound is a narration versus music.

Step 4: Publish Your Presentation

Before finishing your flash video, save your project by selecting **Save** from the **File** menu. Browse to the folder where you wish to save the project, then click on the **Save** button. To save your project as a Flash video select the **Publish** tab (see Figure 5.15). Under the **Publish** tab, the user can adjust options to control how the video will

Figure 5.16. Adobe Photoshop Elements organizer window starting Slide Show.

be saved. First in the **Output Options** section, make sure that the option to **Create Flash File Only** has been selected. Next, in the **Output Settings** section, select the location of where the finished video can be set using the Output folder options, along with adjusting the file name used. When these settings are adjusted to the desired names and locations, click on the **Publish Now!** button to create your video.

The program will display a progress bar to indicate that the video is being created. Once finished there will be a pop-up to allow the user to select to **View Flash Slide Show, Open Output Folder,** or **Upload.** To watch the finished video, click on the option to **View Flash Slide Show,** this will usually open an Internet browser to display the video using your selected theme. The **Open Output Folder** will allow access to the saved files so they can be uploaded to a Web page or transferred to another storage medium,

Figure 5.17. Adobe Photoshop Elements Slide Show Preferences window.

such as a key drive. The **Upload** feature is for sharing created presentations using the SkyAlbum Web site, which requires registering with SkyAlbum to get an account.

PHOTOSHOP ELEMENTS 4.0 AND UP

If you have Photoshop Elements 4.0 and above you can use the program not only to edit and organize your digital pictures, but also to create slide shows in the form of booktalks. The Photoshop Elements program will let you create a presentation that will display images, allow for narration, and even play background music.

To get started creating a booktalk presentation with Photoshop Elements, start the Elements program. Then in the **File** menu, select the option for **Create**, then choose **Slide Show...** (see Figure 5.16).

A new pop-up window for Slide Show Preferences should

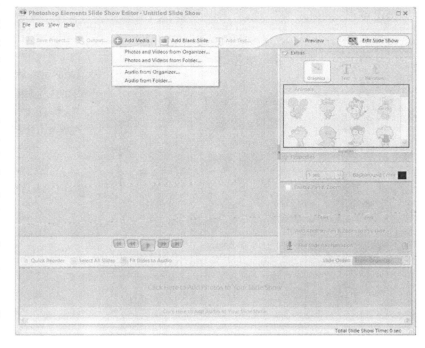

Figure 5.18. Photoshop Elements Slide Show Editor window.

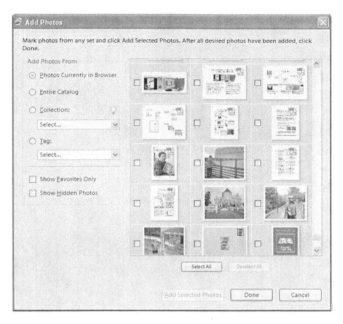

Figure 5.19. Adding images with Elements' Add Photos window.

appear to assist you in getting started with your presentation (see Figure 5.17). Here you can adjust some of the defaults for the presentation, such as how long an image will be displayed, the transitions between slides, and the background color. It is also suggested to at least check the *Apply Pan & Zoom to All Slides* because this feature adjusts the start point and movement of the slide image (like the Ken Burns Effect). If the images already have text or audio captions, they can be included. Once all of the choices have been made, click on the **OK** button.

Step 1: Import Your Images

Next you should see the Slide Show Editor window (see Figure 5.18). Here you can select and organize the pictures for your presentation, set up motion, add narration, and add a soundtrack.

Start creating your booktalk presentation by adding your images using the **Add Media** button. Next select the location where the images are located that you plan to use. Choose the *Organizer* for Elements or browse to a folder. It is possible to add still images and video together, but the video cannot be edited in Elements. Because of the lack of video editing, it is better to use another program to first edit your videos by creating small clips, before you include them.

If you are using the *Organizer* to select your pictures, you will use the *Add Photos* window (see Figure 5.19) to select the images for your booktalk by checking their boxes and then clicking on the **Done** button. If you are browsing to a folder, you can select multiple images by holding down the **Ctrl** key as you click with your mouse on the icon. Once all chosen images have been selected, click the **OK** button to bring the images into the project.

Step 2: Arranging and Adding Titles to Your Pictures

You can arrange the pictures in the order in which you want them to appear in the final booktalk video by dragging the image

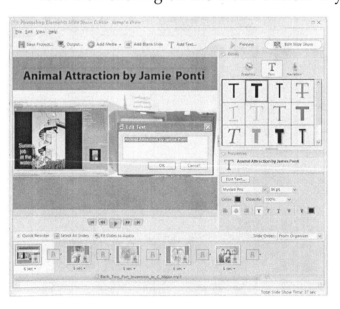

Figure 5.20. Adding text to a slide show in Photoshop Elements.

thumbnails in the bottom section (storyboard) to rearrange them in the sequence you prefer.

Once you have your pictures arranged the way you want them, click on the **Save Project...** button, and then click on the **Next** button.

With the pictures in the project, you can now add titles to the pictures (see Figure 5.20). Add text by first selecting the **Text** button, then either double click on a text type from the display or drag one of the text types onto the screen. You will now have a text box on your preview window where you can type your text. Double click on the text box or select the **Edit Text...** button to start editing. Type the text in the pop-up window titled *Edit Text* (see Figure 5.21). The text you type in the box will appear on the screen in the text box. The titles can be placed in any location on the screen by dragging the text box. You can also change the color, font size, and font type by clicking on the text properties buttons. Click on different thumbnail pictures in the storyboard to add titles to them.

Once you have the titles created, click on the **Save Project...** button and then click on the **Next** button.

Figure 5.21. Edit Text window.

Step 3: Customize Motion and Narrate Your Pictures

In this step you can add your own audio track and decide how you want your pictures to move and change. Each picture can have its own audio recording and individual movement.

Movement

By default each picture added to the show is displayed for five seconds before changing to the next. You can change this timing for any picture by clicking on the display time below the thumbnail image in the storyboard and either picking from the available list of times or choosing the **Custom** option. When customizing the time for display, the limits are 0.5 to 120 seconds.

You can also use this option to control the picture's motion.

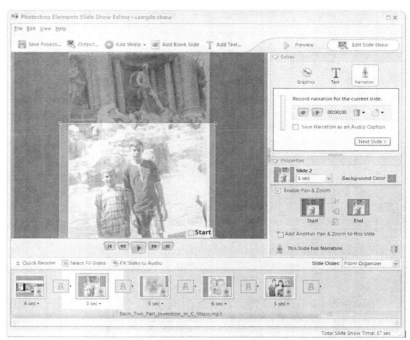

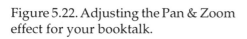
Figure 5.22. Adjusting the Pan & Zoom effect for your booktalk.

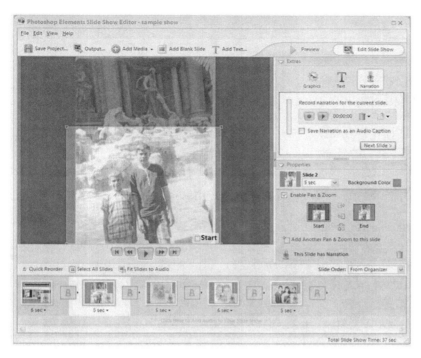

Figure 5.23. Adding narration to your booktalk.

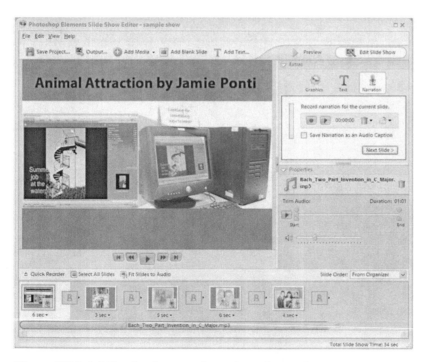

Figure 5.24. Adding background music to the project.

Here you can adjust the portion of the image to display at the start and at the end of the picture viewing time. The computer will create a motion effect between the two settings. For example, you could set the picture to start on a small section and then zoom out to display the whole image. To change the size or direction of motion, first select the image from the storyboard at the bottom of the window. Then in the Properties section, with the Enable Pan & Zoom checked, select one of the two small images in the box (**Start or End image**). When selected, the preview window will display the portion of the image that will actually be visible (see Figure 5.22). Adjust the size by clicking and dragging the corner boxes to the desired size. Adjust the position by clicking and dragging the image box to the desired location. Now select End image and adjust its size and position. The video display will be a smooth zooming transition from the Start selection to the End selection. You can select any picture in the presentation to change the motion or duration from the default settings.

Between each image in the storyboard is a box that indicates the type of transition between the images. Clicking on the small arrow to the right of the box allows the user to change the transition effect between pictures. The default is a fade, but each picture can have its own transition from the 24 available options. Once you have your motions and transitions set, click on the **Save Project...** button to save your work.

Audio Narration

You should first write your script and decide which part of the script goes with each picture. You will need a microphone connected to your computer. To start the process of adding your voice to your booktalk, select the **Narration** button from the top right of the window. Notice under the **Narration** button there is a recording area. When you are ready to record, click on the picture to which you want to add your narration, and then click on the red **record** button (see Figure 5.23). When you have finished adding the narration for that image, click on the **stop** button. If you make mistakes, you can click the trash can and choose **Delete This Narration** before starting the narration again for the image. Selecting the button above the storyboard **Fit Slides to Audio** will adjust the display time for the images to match your recording time. Click on a different thumbnail picture or use the **Next Slide]** button to change to another image and add a new narration.

Once you have the movements, transitions, and narrations set, save your project.

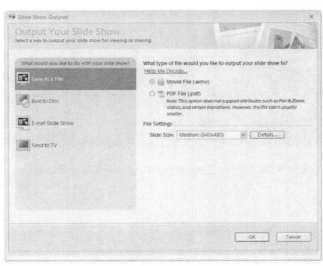

Figure 5.25. Selecting the file settings for the created video file.

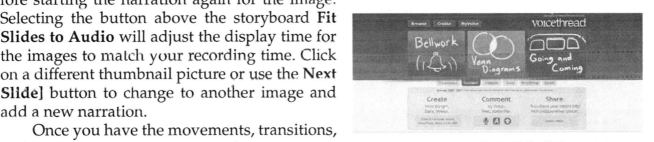

Figure 5.26. VoiceThread Web site (http://www.voicethread.com).

Step 4: Add Background Music

In addition to the narration for each slide, a soundtrack can also be added to your booktalk by selecting from music saved on your computer. Elements' slideshow can use audio files in mp3, WAV, or WMA formats. Click on either the *Click Here to Add Audio to your Slide Show* bar at the bottom of the window or the **Add Media** button at the top of the screen, and then select the *Organizer* or browse to your music. Once your have selected your music, click

Figure 5.27. Using the Create option in Voicethread.

on the OK button to add it to your booktalk presentation. The music will now spread across the entire project. Click once on the soundtrack bar to access the sound properties (see Figure 5.24). You should now adjust the volume setting of the background music. We suggest that you set volume at half or lower so that it doesn't interfere with the spoken narration.

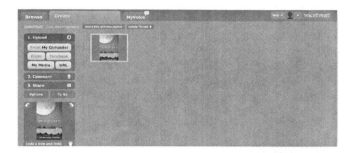

Figure 5.28. Uploading an image into VoiceThread.

Figure 5.29. Recording a comment in VoiceThread.

Figure 5.30. Setting the sharing of a VoiceThread booktalk.

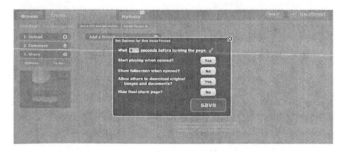

Figure 5.31. Setting the play options for a Voice-Thread.

In the preview section, click on the play button to preview your movie. Once you have the background music set, save your project.

Step 5: Save Your Booktalk

Save your booktalk project as a movie file (*.wmv), starting with selecting **Output Slide Show…** from the **File** menu. At this stage, the program will create a separate movie file from the project file that you created. While Elements offers a variety of options, we suggest that you use the **Save As a File** option (see Figure 5.25). You can adjust the *File Setting* for the finished size of the video. We recommend either **High (800 × 600)** or **Medium (640 × 480)** as initial choices. Understand that the larger screen setting will cause the movie to have a larger file size. If you are planning to create a Video CD to play your booktalks on a television, you should choose that option. The smallest file size would be the one for e-mail, but this one would also have the least clarity.

Once you have made your selection, click on the OK button to start the file conversion process. The program turns your project into a movie file and saves it. You can play your booktalk movie using Window's Media Player or any other program that will play .wmv files such as Real Player and QuickTime (with the wmv plug in).

VOICETHREAD

A *VoiceThread* is an online media album that allows viewers to add comments, collaborate, or just share, in audio or text form. This application allows an entire group's stories to be created and collected in one place.

VoiceThread allows you to record single or multiple voices and images to create a multimedia show that is personalized and applicable for educational projects such as booktalks. Your VoiceThread presentations can be made public to anyone, or you can make them accessible only to selected individuals. You can even set up an account for individual classes that will allow multiple classmates access to the account for group projects! You can also embed your Voice-Thread presentations in your blogs. Visitors to your VoiceThread can comment on your booktalk. It is truly a social application.

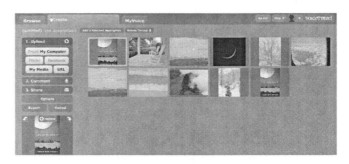

Figure 5.32. Preparing to comment on a VoiceThread booktalk.

VoiceThread is accessed at http://www.voicethread.com (see Figure 5.26). Registration is free to educators.

Step by Step

1. Register, and then apply for a free educator account by clicking the **Go Pro** button in the main header of the site. Click the **K–12 Educator** link and fill out the form. After you click the link in a confirmation e-mail message, you will be ready to begin VoiceThreading.

2. Go to the Create page of the Voice-Thread Web site and make the Voice-Thread by importing and arranging images, documents, presentations, or short videos (see Figure 5.27).

Figure 5.33. Animoto playing a booktalk on Dairy Queen.

Navigate to the folder on your computer or attached storage drive that contains your pictures. Click on **Upload.** You can upload from your computer or from Flickr, Facebook, and other sites.

The uploaded picture shows in VoiceThread (see Figure 5.28). At this point, you have the option of rotating the picture if needed. You can also add a title and link.

Figure 5.34. Animoto Web site (http://www.animoto.com).

3. Add audio using the program's tools. Click on **Comment.** Your picture will appear with a button to allow you to record your comment. Click on the record button, record your narration, and click **Stop Recording** when finished (see Figure 5.29). Do this for each of the pictures in your thread.

4. When you are finished recording your thread, you can set the options for sharing. You can keep your thread private or share with others (see Figure 5.30).

Figure 5.35. Completing the Animoto sign up process.

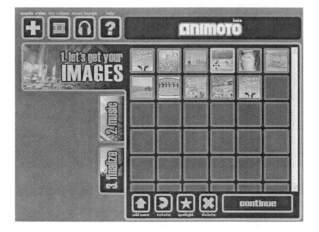

Figure 5.36. Adding images to your presentation in Animoto.

5. You now can choose options for sharing your thread (see Figure 5.31). This is where you can set a time for each picture to be shown. You can also choose to play the thread in fullscreen mode and decide whether you want others to be able to share your images.

6. K–7 students (13 and under) should only participate using "identities," which are extra "faces" on the teacher's account and consist of nothing more than a picture and a first name. The picture does not need to be a face photo at all but only needs to represent the student so he or she can recognize his or her "mark." Open your VoiceThread and click on the Avatar next to the left arrow and then select "Create another identity." Add a new identity for each student.

7. Have your students prepare their booktalk, and then record it on the slides in their thread.

8. Now when you are viewing the VoiceThread and one of the students wants to comment on a particular image, click the Avatar next to the left arrow and then choose that child's identity. Now they are set up to comment (see Figure 5.32).

ANIMOTO

Animoto is a Web application that renders unique photo montages using impressive motion graphics, effects, and transitions from photos and music/audio that you upload (see Figure 5.33). The software will render something unique on each pass, and the results will be radically different depending on the style of audio you choose. A fast-paced rock audio will create a fast-paced video, while a narrative will result in a slower video. The free videos are limited to 30 seconds, so the booktalks will need to be very quick and simple. Longer videos can be created for a cost.

To use Animoto, you need to register. Go to http://www.animoto.com and sign up for a free account (see Figure 5.34).

Figure 5.37. Uploading the audio track to Animoto.

You will need to supply your e-mail address and choose a user name and password. Click on the **sign up** link to get started, and then fill in the required information (see Figure 5.35).

Now you are all set to create your Animoto video. You should storyboard the video and prepare the script in advance. You need a minimum of 10 images to create an Animoto video. Your audio can be no more than 30 seconds. Although you can use a music track, for a booktalk you should record your booktalk using other software and save it as an mp3 file (see Chapter 6 for more information on recording audio).

Figure 5.38. Finishing your video presentation with Animoto.

Once the images are saved and the audio is recorded, you are ready to make your Animoto video.

Step 1: Upload the images for your presentation, and then arrange them (see Figure 5.36).

Step 2: Upload your booktalk audio mp3 file by clicking on the upload button and then browsing to and choosing the file (see Figure 5.37).

Step 3: Finalize your video. It may take a few minutes to render your video depending on how many pictures you use. You will need to give your presentation a name, description, and your name (see Figure 5.38).

Finally, sit back and enjoy your presentation.

REFERENCE

American Association of School Librarians (AASL). (2007). AASL Standards for the 21st-Century Learner. Retrieved May 3, 2008, from http://www.ala.org/ala/aasl/aaslprof tools/learningstandards/AASL_Learning_Standards_2007.pdf.

6

Audio Booktalks

One of the technologies that appeals to students is audio technology. Audio booktalks include digital audio recordings available online, commonly called podcasts, and audio CD collections of the digital audio recordings. To create audio booktalks, a computer, microphone, and software that can be obtained freely on the Internet are the necessary tools.

IN THE CLASSROOM

Ms. Jefferson is a reading coach for a school housing grades 6–12 located in a rural part of her state. In her job as a reading or literacy coach, she assists in student assessment and provides instruction, sometimes to students herself but often in partnership with the classroom teacher, and she offers leadership, usually in the forms of professional development and mentoring. Currently, she is working with Ms. Koontz, a second-year teacher who has requested assistance and suggestions for improving her classroom activities with reading. Ms. Koontz's students participate in a pull out program using the five student computers in her room and a laptop for teacher use (see Figure 6.1). Her students need reading remediation or recovery. Together Ms. Jefferson and Ms. Koontz work with the school librarian Jason Wu and plan to team teach a reading unit focused on comprehension that will use the literature circle to help develop student abilities. Before the start of the unit the students use an interest inventory to identify their areas of interest to help in tailoring book selections, which is then analyzed by the three educators. Based on the inventories, the topic selected for the reading is survival in nature, and the books available to the students for their reading groups include *Hatchet*, *My Side of the Mountain*, and *Wild Man Island*. Mr. Wu assembles sets of each book and provides a modified book introduction to each of the books. Ms. Jefferson has noticed that the students all have personal mp3 players, so working with Mr. Wu, she incorporates them into the lessons. She plays chapter excerpts from sites such as Scholastic.com as well as mp3 files from the library media center collection to encourage interest and to provide a "voice" to the books. Together with Ms. Koontz, she also informs the students that at the end of the book the students will create their own podcast instead of writing a report. This podcast will be a booktalk that will be placed on the school library site.

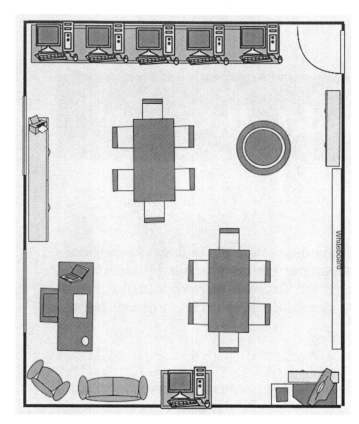

Figure 6.1. Ms. Koontz's classroom setup.

Excerpt: Reading Coach Calendar (Table 6.1)

Reading Coach: J. Jefferson

School: Stonyground Middle School (Region 6)

PDS—Professional Development Support Calendar

Standards (IRA/NCTE)

2—Students read a wide range of literature from many periods in many genres to build an understanding of the many dimensions of human experience.

11—Students participate as knowledgeable, reflective, creative, and critical members of a variety of literacy communities.

12—Students use spoken, written, and visual language to accomplish their own purposes.

LESSON SEQUENCE

- Assess students using reading interest inventory.
- Based on results, work with library media specialist to create reading collection.
- Students form reading groups based on book selection.
- Students take part in standard literature circle activities on a daily basis.
- As culminating activity students working in cooperative groups will develop digital audio file booktalks on computers in classroom.

Lesson Plan—Podcasting Booktalks

Lesson Title: Podcasting Booktalks for Students

Purpose/Outcomes/Objectives:

The purpose of this lesson is to practice public speaking and persuasion. Students will create a podcast presenting a booktalk as a favorite book. The booktalk will be recorded by the student. Students will then use audio editing software to edit the booktalk. Students will work in teams on the editing of the audio file. The teams will create a group audio file of all the booktalks from the team. The overall goal of the booktalk is to persuade the audience to read the book. The final projects will be posted for the entire class to share.

Table 6.1
Reading Coach Calendar

TARGET GROUP/ TEACHER	ACTION PLAN BASED ON NEEDS ASSESSMENT	IMPLEMENTATION (Include date and time)	FOLLOW-UP (Include date and time)
Ms. Koontz (Skills 6-7-8)	Students assigned to class based on state reading assessment scores of less than 3.	Date: 10/3/07 Time: 1:15—2:00	Date: 10/5/07 Time:
	Teacher asked for assistance for low student interest.	Observed class working on reading skills including comprehension and vocabulary.	Team teach during introduction of new reading materials and literature circle.
		Observed all students having iPods or other mp3 players.	Follow-up with team teaching conclusion lesson following next reading with students creating audio-based booktalks as writing alternative
		Additional targeted high-interest reading materials based on student interests are needed. Suggest implementation of literature circle for reading activity.	
		Date: 10/5/7–10/20/07 **Lesson Sequence**	Date: 10/5/7–10/20/07 For each session, model teaching and activities, then monitor teacher as that day's lesson is delivered.
		• Assess students using reading interest inventory.	
		• Based on results, work with library media specialist to create reading collection.	
		• Students form reading groups based on book selection.	
		• Students take part in standard literature circle activities on daily basis.	
		• As culminating activity, students working in cooperative groups will develop digital audio file booktalks on computers in classroom.	

Standards Addressed:

AASL

1.1.2 Use prior and background knowledge as a context for new learning.

2.1.4 Use technology and other information tools to analyze and organize information.

3.1.2 Participate and collaborate as members of a social and intellectual network of learners.

4.4.1 Identify own areas of interest.

English Language Arts

Writing:

LA.8.3.1.1—generating ideas from multiple sources based upon teacher-directed topics and personal interests;

LA.8.3.1.2—making a plan for writing that addresses purpose, audience, main idea, logical sequence, and time frame for completion;

LA.8.3.5.1—prepare writing using technology in a format appropriate to audience;

LA.8.3.5.3—share the writing with the intended audience.

Media Literacy:

LA.8.6.3.2—demonstrate the ability to select and ethically use print and nonprint media appropriate for the purpose, occasion, and audience to develop into a formal presentation;

Technology:

LA.8.6.4.1—use appropriate available technologies to enhance communication and achieve a purpose (e.g., video, digital technology); and

LA.8.6.4.2—evaluate and apply digital tools to publications and presentations.

ISTE Technology:

Basic Operations and Concepts:

The student will demonstrate proficiency in the use of technology.

Social and Ethical Issues:

The student will practice responsible use of technology systems, information, and software.

The student will demonstrate knowledge of technologies that support collaboration, personal pursuits, and productivity.

Technology Research Tools:

The student will evaluate and select new information resources and techno-logical innovations based on the appropriateness for specific tasks.

Technology Communication Tools:

The student will use a variety of media and formats to communicate infor-mation and ideas effectively to multiple audiences.

Tools and Resources:

Software:

- Audio Recording Software GarageBand (Mac); Audacity (PC/Mac/Linux); or equivalent software;
- Word processing software, such as Microsoft Word;
- CD or iTunes (optional).

Hardware:

- Computer
- headset microphone

Preparation:

Technology/Classroom Management Strategies:

This lesson will be presented to the class by the teacher and the library media spe-cialist. Each student will meet with the teacher/library media specialist to discuss their title selection and to brainstorm talking points. Students will need to choose at least one book they have read and wish to share with other students.

Lesson Development

The students will be presented with examples of podcasts. The podcasts will origi-nate from a variety of sources. Students will choose examples that appeal to them and take notes on why the podcast was successful. (See later in this chapter for example Web sites.)

Instructional Activity:

1. Teacher/library media specialist will model how to record and save a pod-cast.
2. Teacher/library media specialist will help students develop scripts. The scripting will be facilitated using questioning techniques to help students to discover an effective way to "sell" their book.
3. Teacher/library media specialist will work with students through the cre-ation of a podcast.

Process:

1. Student will choose a book they wish to share.
2. Student will write a script (storyboard) showcasing their book choice.

3. Student will end their script with a closing comment to encourage others to read the book (the hook).

4. Student will peer review their scripts.

5. Teacher/library media specialist will present a mini-lesson on the use of recording software.

6. Students will practice recording their script using software until they feel they have met the rubric standards for oral presentation.

7. Students will add music to the beginning and ending of their podcast. They can bring in a CD of the music to download. (This step is optional. It will be based on the time constraints of the students.)

8. Students will save the podcast for future listening.

Closure:

Students will present their podcasts to the class. Podcasts may be made available via the school Web page as appropriate.

Evaluation Procedure:

The rubric will be shared with students prior to the implementation of the lesson. (Table 6.2)

Booktalk Podcast Rubric

CATEGORY	4	2	1
Storyline/Plot	Establishes a purpose early on and maintains a clear focus throughout. Podcast has a clear beginning, middle, and end.	There are a few lapses in focus, but the purpose is fairly clear. Podcast lacks a clear beginning, middle, and end.	It is difficult to figure out the purpose of the podcast. Podcast scenes do not comprise a complete story.
Point of View— Awareness of Audience	Strong awareness of audience in the design. Clear understanding of why vocabulary, audio, and hook fit the target audience.	Some awareness of audience in the design. Difficult to explain why vocabulary, audio, and hook fit the target audience.	Limited awareness of the needs and interests of the target audience.
Audio	Voice over recording is clear and audible. Music is appropriate and stirs a rich emotional response that matches the story line well.	Voice over recording is somewhat unclear and barely audible. Some music is appropriate but may be distracting and does not add much to the story.	Voice over recording is unclear and inaudible. Music is not appropriate and is distracting, inappropriate, OR was not used.
Editing	Podcast demonstrates careful editing of audio. Completed podcast includes information about the title, author, and publication of the book being used.	Podcast demonstrates little editing of audio. Completed podcast has incomplete information about the title, author, and publication of the book being used.	Podcast demonstrates poor editing of audio. Completed podcast lacks information about the book being used.

From *Tech-Savvy Booktalkers: A Guide for 21st-Century Educators* by Nancy J. Keane and Terence W. Cavanaugh. Westport, CT: Libraries Unlimited. Copyright © 2009.

CREATING AN AUDIO BOOKTALK

There are a number of different kinds of audio files in common use. For this section, we will be discussing two common formats: the CD audio format and the mp3 file. Both of these formats can be used effectively to produce quality audio booktalks that can be played later. What you would like to do with your technology-enhanced booktalks will determine the format that you wish to make. If you are planning on distributing your audio booktalks over the Internet or through some other form of file server then you will most likely want them in mp3 format. If you are planning on playing your audio booktalks on a CD player, then you will need CD audio formatted files and blank CDs. Our suggestion is to create your audio booktalks in mp3 format first and then convert the files to CD audio format if desired (see "Converting Files to CD Audio" later in this chapter).

When starting to create your own audio recordings, we recommend using a program such as Audacity, or GarageBand if it is already installed on your Apple computer. Audacity is an open source audio recording application with a full set of editing features and a relatively simple interface and runs on Windows, Macintosh, and Linux platforms. It can also create mp3-format audio for distributing (such as for a podcast). If you don't already have this program you will need to download and install Audacity from the Sourceforge Web site (http://audacity.sourceforge.net/), along with the program be sure to download the LAME mp3 encoder from the site and save it to a location that you can remember—you will need to point the Audacity program to that files location the first time that you create an mp3 file.

Step 1: Before You Record

If you have the software there are still a few things to do before you begin recording your booktalk. First, you should plan your narrative, such as by writing a script or creating an outline. In addition to the software you will need to connect a microphone to your computer (see Chapter 7 for more information on microphones). The microphone will need to be connected to the microphone-in connection on your computer, which could be on the front, side, or back. Also, you should use headphones, and they will need to be connected also.

Once you start the Audacity program it is important to make sure that the microphone is selected as the recording source. There is a drop-down menu in the mixer toolbar, if it does not already show "Microphone," click on the down arrow and select it (see Figure 6.2).

Next you will need to set the recording preferences. Open the Audacity **Preferences** window from the **Edit** menu (or press Ctrl-p). On the first tab, *Audio I/O*, verify that your sound card is selected as the device for both playback and recording. In the *Channels* drop-down box under *Recording*, choose 1 (Mono). As you are

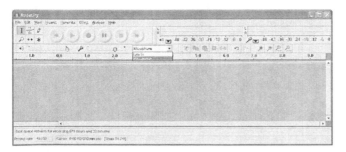

Figure 6.2. Make sure that the Microphone is set as the recording source in Audacity.

most likely only using one microphone, *Mono* is sufficient. Use the *Stereo* option if you have a computer that allows you to connect two microphones. If you are not using two microphones, selecting the Stereo option will simply cause the mono track to be duplicated, which increases the final file size without adding any advantages. On the next tab, *Quality*, for voice recording it is sufficient to set the *Default Sample Rate* to 44,100 Hz and the *Default Sample Format* to 16-bit (see Figure 6.3). Now select the File Formats tab, set the *MP3 Export Setup* to a *Bit Rate* of 64. For voice-recorded audio a setting of 64 should be sufficient, but if you want a higher quality recording set it at 128. Don't worry about the rest of the settings, click on the **OK** button to exit the Preferences window.

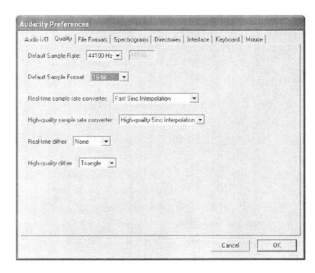

Figure 6.3. Audacity Preferences Quality settings for sample rate and bit rate.

Step 2: Recording Your Booktalk

Once your microphone has been connected, click on the microphone icon in Audacity's Meter toolbar to turn on monitoring. This will cause the indicator level (red bar) to begin moving slightly as the system detects the room noise (see Figure 6.4). Now talk into your microphone with your normal voice and make adjustments to the Microphone Input Volume, adjusting it so that the red bar moves close to the right edge of the meter without getting all the way to

Figure 6.4. Monitoring the input sound using Audacity's Meter toolbar.

the edge. If the input goes too far to the right the recording will be clipped, causing the recording to be distorted. When you have adjusted the level so that the input is loud enough without being too loud, you're ready to record.

Before recording your actual booktalk you might want to make a practice recording to get used to the controls. To record your voice push the **Recording** button (red circle) (see Figure 6.5). Instead of pressing the Stop button (black square) when you need a break press the **Pause** button (double blue line), press the **Stop** button only when you have finished. Every time that you press the stop button and then the record button, a new track is made (this is actually not a problem because when you are finished all the tracks will be collapsed into a single track). Also, if you make a mistake,

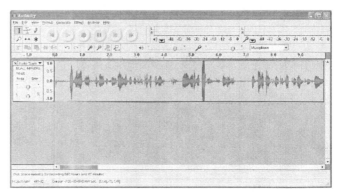

Figure 6.5. Using Audacity to record a booktalk.

Audio Recording Tips

LibriVox (http://librivox.org/), an all-volunteer audio book site, offers these tips for recording read-out-loud materials.

- Read first, record second. It always helps to know your material before you set out to record it.
- Talk slowly. Set a pace that seems almost unnaturally slow to you.
- Pause. Take breaks between sentences and paragraphs.
- Enunciate. Treasure every syllable.
- Modulate. Monotones are evil. Bring life and vitality to what you are reading.

mispronounce something, cough, or even laugh, that is OK, you don't have to stop and start over again. Now press the **Play** button (green triangle) to see how well your recording worked. If you don't want to include your mistake, just repeat what you would have said and then edit out your mistake later.

If you don't like the track you just made or you only made it for practice click on the "X" next to the Audio Track.

Now it is time to create your audio booktalk. Push the **Record** button and start booktalking. When you finish recording your booktalk, press the yellow square **Stop** button and then save the file by selecting **File** from the menu and then choosing **Save Project** (Ctrl+s). The project file is saved in an .AUP format, which is only used with the Audacity program.

Step 3: Editing Your Booktalk

Now listen to the recording that you made. It may be fine, in which case no editing will be needed. But if you find that there are some problems, such as a repeated word, large pauses, or you added in filler words such as "umm" and "you know," these things can be edited out. Editing out an error can be as simple as listening to the recording to find the problem, then highlighting it and pressing your delete button or choosing **Delete** from the **Edit** menu (see Figure 6.6). The program is also very powerful, and you can do advanced editing, such as adding a music track and inserting other audio clips, such as sound effects, into your booktalk.

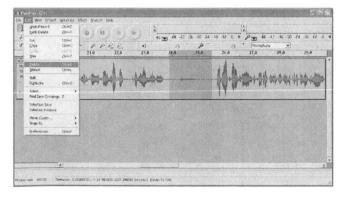

Figure 6.6. Deleting a sound from a recording using Audacity.

Step 4: Creating the mp3 File

After you have edited your booktalk recording and are satisfied, you should now save the audio recording as an mp3 file for playback or distribution. To save your booktalk recording as an mp3, open the **File** menu, and then choose the option to **Export As MP3...**(see Figure 6.7). Use the save window to save your file to a location, and then click on the **Save** button. If your program has not already been linked to the LAME mp3 encoder (lame_enc. dll) you will need to locate the file for the

program before you can continue. Use the
browsing window to find the lame_enc.dll
file and then click on the **Open** button.

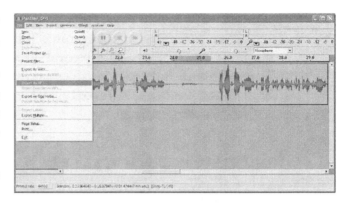

The last step is to edit the ID3 tags for
the mp3 file. A pop-up window will provide
you with the template for how to add the
ID3 tags. We suggest that you do the following in each of the blanks (see Figure 6.8):

- In the *Title* section add the title of the
  book,
- for the *Artist* the author,

Figure 6.7. Creating an mp3 audio file with Audacity.

- For the *Album*, use "Booktalks" as an
  album name
- Add a *Track Number* if you like
- For the *Year*, write in the year the book
  was written
- For *Genre*, select the option for *Speech*
- And under *Comments*, write in the name
  of the person giving the booktalk.

This information, such as the title and artist, will be displayed by the media player when
the mp3 audio file is being played.

You can take the ID3 tags even further by
using an mp3 player such as Windows Media
Player or iTunes. For example, open the file
with Windows Media Player, right-click on the
file name in the *Now Playing* list and choose **Advanced Tag Editor.** The Title and Artist fields
should already be filled in, but if they are not
you can fill them in now. One great thing to do
is add a picture of the book or of the booktalker
holding the book that will then be displayed
when the file is played. First save a picture of
the book's cover on your computer. Then in the
Advanced Tag Editor, select the Pictures tab,

Figure 6.8. Adding ID3 tag to an mp3 recording.

now click on the **Add...** button. Browse to where you saved the book cover image,
and then click on the **Open** button. You can select the picture type if you like, but most
likely *Cover* will be best, and then click on the **OK** button to save your cover image with
the mp3 file.

Tutorials and Resources

Audacity FAQ: http://librivox.org/wiki/moin.cgi/Audacity
Audacity Tutorial for Podcasters (videos): http://www.how-to-podcast-tutorial.
com

Audacity **Tutorial:** http://clk.about.com/?zi=1/XJ&sdn=radio&zu=http%3A%2F
%2Faudacity.sourceforge.net%2Fhelp%2Ftutorials
Audacity: http://Audacity.sourceforge.net
Lame Encoder: http://mitiok.free.fr
LibriVox Newbie Guide to Recording: http://librivox.org/wiki/moin.cgi/Newbie
GuideToRecording

PODCASTING BOOKTALKS

Now that you have created an audio booktalk, it is time to share it. These created audio files can be put onto CD for playing in classrooms or at home, played in a computer in the library, or played in commons areas around the school, such as the hallway in front of the library or the front office. Students often feel differently and work much harder on projects that they will know will be going outside of the classroom or school. One thing that can be done for sharing the audio booktalks is to put the mp3 files online for sharing and even go so far as to create a booktalking podcast. Podcasting is a method of publishing audio files that listeners can subscribe to, which are then played on the listener's computer or mp3 player. These subscribed users will automatically receive the podcasts as part of their online news subscription. The files can also be available to others who visit a Web page that has the links for each of the files.

If you are going to publish the files online, they can be posted anywhere on your Web site, but it is usually best to put them all into one directory on the Web server, making them easier to find and manage. You might want to use a common file naming structure, such as including the book title and who is creating the booktalk (ex: title_reader.mp3). Next you should think about where you want to share the files. One method is to host the file on a Web page, such as part of the school library's site that has links to each of the audio files. Another method is to share the audio booktalks as podcasts, which will require a newsfeed. A newsfeed uses an RSS file (Rich Site Summary, or Really Simple Syndication) to inform the subscriber that there is a new file or posting available. With the booktalk podcast placed on an Internet server, such as the one hosting the school or library Web page, use a blogging tool, such as Google's Blogger (www.blogger.com), to create a blog posting for each mp3 file you create. Within the blog post create a link to the URL of the podcast.

Figure 6.9. Librarian Sonja Cole, Bookwink's host and booktalker (http://www.bookwink.com).

Posting Your Booktalk as a Podcast

You will need a blog account, such as with Blogger, along with your mp3 booktalking file placed as an mp3 file online. If you do not have a Blogger account you can go to the Blogger site (www.blogger.com) and create one for no charge. (See Chapter 3 for more information.)

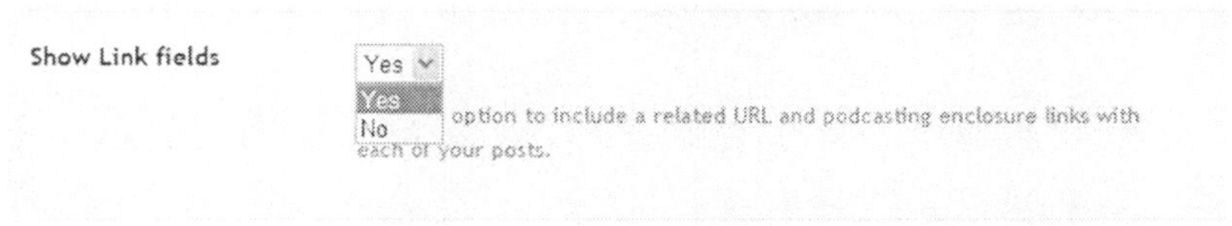

Go to your *Blogger* page and login to begin your posting.

Figure 6.10. Changing the Formatting Settings so that link fields will show. Copyright © 2007 Google Blogger™ Web publishing service.

If you are using one of Blogger's layouts or a classic template for your blog, go to the *Settings* tab. Under the *Settings* tab, select the *Formatting* tab. Next scroll down the page and find the options for setting the *Show Link Field*. Set the *Show Link Field* to **Yes** and then click on the **Save** button (see Figure 6.10).

Next click on the *Posting* tab, which should present you with a blank posting template. Select the link to **Add enclosure link.** This action will open up a new section. Write in or paste the Web address for your audio booktalk into the Link and the Enclosures fields. The system will automatically recognize the MIME type, so you shouldn't have to write anything there. Also write a brief description about your podcast in the *Compose* window (see Figure 6.11). If you have an image, such as the book cover or the person giving the booktalk, use the image tool to add the image from your computer or paste in a URL linking to the location where a picture is posted on the Web. When your blog/podcast is complete click on the **Publish Post** button.

Check your blog by browsing to your blog page or clicking on the View Blog link. The title of the posting will become a clickable link that will pull up and play the mp3 booktalk file that was placed online (see Figure 6.12).

When your blog subscribers view or receive the page in their RSS readers, such as Google Reader, your booktalk recording will appear as embedded audio.

Examples of Booktalk Podcasts

Bookwink: http://www.bookwink.com

Bookwink's mission is "to inspire kids to read, through podcasting and Web video" (see Figure 6.9). Designed for students grades 3 through 8 with books that will make them excited about reading. The presented videos are short (about 3 minutes) and are updated monthly.

Booktalks Quick and Simple: http://nancykeane.com/rss.html

Provides a daily podcast featuring a quick booktalk. Each of the talks lasts about a minute and features titles for all grades. Visit the site or subscribe via RSS.

Just One More Book: http://www.justonemorebook.com

A nonprofit effort celebrating "literacy and great children's books." This site has booktalks ranging in length from 5 to 35 minutes that are recorded in a "coffee shop somewhere in Canada."

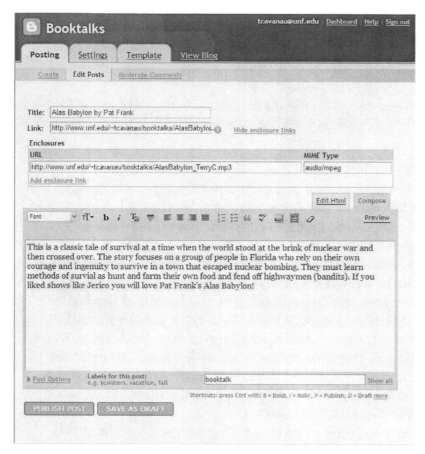

Figure 6.11. Creating your booktalk podcast posting. Copyright © 2007 Google Blogger™ Web publishing service.

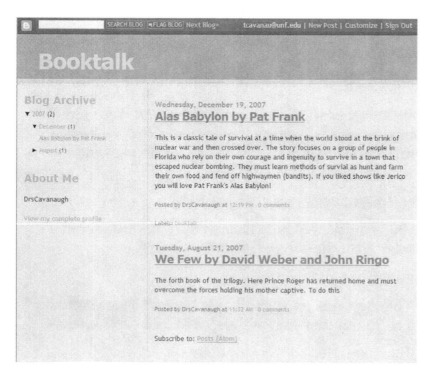

Nancy Pearl's Book Reviews: http://kuow.org/search.php?get=1&slShowSearch=NP

These book reviews (booktalks) are made for Puget Sound Public Radio and are archived as mp3 files each Monday. The collection includes a variety of books from thrillers to memoirs, internationalfictiontooverlooked authors, and young adult novels.

And among the growing number of student-created book talks out there are:

- **Readers Circle Booktalks** (Pike School): http://web.mac.com/pikeschool/iWeb/library/Readers%20Circle%20Booktalks/Readers%20Circle%20Booktalks.html
- **Runkle School Book Reviews:**http://www.runkle.org/Podcasts/index.html
- **Portland Public Schools:** http://ppsmultimedialibrary.blogspot.com/search/label/Podcasts

Publishers podcast, too. Simon and Schuster offer its **SimonSays Podcasts** (http://www.simonsays.com/content/consumer.cfm?app=podcast_archive).

Figure 6.12. Finished blog/podcast page. Copyright © 2007 Google Blogger™ Web publishing service.

Resources

About: Podcast Basics with tutorials: http://podcasting.about.com/od/podcastbasic1/Podcast_Basics.htm

Blogger Help: http://help.blogger.com

ENHANCED PODCASTS

Another way to make your audio booktalk is to use Apple's GarageBand if you have a Macintosh computer. The GarageBand program is well-suited

To save a presentation as images:

In PowerPoint, select **Save As** from the **File** menu. In the *Save As* window change the *Save as type:* drop-down to a desired image format (JPEG, GIF, or PING). Also in the *Save As* window, locate where you want to save your presentation images, and then click on the **Save** button. Next the program will prompt you with a question about saving every slide or only the current slide as an image. Make your selection by clicking on the appropriate button, and the program will create a new folder in the location you chose with all your new presentation images.

In Impress select Export As from the File menu. In the Export window change the File format: drop-down to a desired image format (BMP, JPEG, GIF, PCT, TIFF, plus more that are rarely used). The selection option in the Export window is only used for saving a selected portion of a slide. Also in the Export window, locate where you want to save your presentation images. The best place to put your images is in a new folder. Then click on the Save button. This will save just the current slide as an image; you will need to export each slide to convert the whole presentation into images.

for creating podcasts and can even create enhanced podcasts. An enhanced podcast is a podcast that also includes images or video, titles, chapter markers, and Web links with the audio. When someone listens to the enhanced podcast on a computer or other handheld player with a video screen, its pictures will be shown in a slideshow format.

For your enhanced podcast you should create or find a collection of images. One option is to create images using a program such as Microsoft's PowerPoint or Open Office's Impress. In either of these two programs, create your slideshow, and then save the finished presentation slides as images.

Once you have created your audio recording in GarageBand, click and drag the images to the Podcast Track to include them in your podcast. Once the images are in the track, the edges of each picture space can be dragged to either lengthen or shorten the amount of time that the image is displayed (see Figure 6.13). When you have finished editing your enhanced podcast, save it as an .mp4. These files can then be burned onto a CD, played on a computer, or shared via a Web server. If you want to share your files though a service such as iTunes, they will first need to be placed online.

Web Resources

Apple's GarageBand Tutorials: http://www.apple.com/support/ilife/tutorials/garageband/index.html

Figure 6.13. Editing the display time for a podcast image in GarageBand.

Apple's GarageBand Manuals: http://docs.info.apple.com/article.html?artnum= 93615

ComTechLab's Introducing GarageBand: http://comtechlab.iupui.edu/tutori alsfolder/garageband.html

Expert Village's GarageBand Tutorials: http://www.expertvillage.com/videos/ apple-garageband-enhanced-podcast.htm

Penn State's GarageBand 3 Creating a Podcast: http://podcasts.psu.edu/files/ GarageBandPodcast.pdf

CONVERTING FILES TO CD AUDIO

The odds are that you already have a program that will convert your mp3 files to CD audio and place them on a disc for you. This process is called burning a CD, and programs such as Window's Media Player or iTunes can be used to do it. Before you start, check to see that your computer has a disc drive that can burn discs and is not just a player/reader drive.

Creating an Audio CD with Windows Media Player

1. Start Windows Media Player and then click on the *Burn* tab. Note that there is also a small arrow just below the *Burn* tab: Make sure that the audio CD is the type selected.
2. You will also need to insert a blank CD disc into your computer's CD burning drive. We suggest just using CD-R discs as in the process of burning all data will be required to be erased.
3. Next, drag the files that you want to save on the CD from your library or a folder, and drop them onto the *List* pane on the right hand side. This will create the list of files to burn.

    A standard audio CD has a time capacity limit of between 70 and 80 minutes of audio content. The Player automatically calculates how many minutes and seconds of empty space remain on the disc after each song is added to the burn list and inserts two seconds between songs when burning. If you plan for a maximum total of about 70 minutes, you should be fine.

4. You can adjust the play list by dragging files up or down in the *Burn* list to arrange them in the order you want them to occur on the CD.
5. Once you have all your files in order, click the **Start Burn** button at the bottom of the *Burn* list panel (see Figure 6.14).

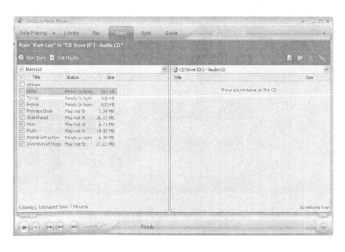

Figure 6.14. Burning audio booktalks onto an audio CD with Windows Media Player.

6. When the CD is finished being burned, the disc drive will automatically open. Your audio CD is now ready for playing.

Figure 6.15. Burning audio booktalks onto an audio CD with iTunes.

Creating an Audio CD with iTunes

1. With iTunes running, create a new playlist (**File > New Playlist**). Your new playlist should be on the left hand side of the iTunes display. You can rename this playlist by clicking on the playlist that appears.
2. Select the booktalks that you want to burn onto the CD by holding down the Ctrl key and clicking on the tracks that you want. To deselect a track, continue holding Ctrl and simply click on the booktalk title again.
3. Once all desired tracks have been selected, release the Ctrl key and drag the files over to the new playlist that you created.
4. Insert a blank CD-R into the burning drive, and wait for the disc to be recognized.
5. In the playlist folder that you created, there will be a **Burn CD** button at the top right of iTunes: Click on this button to start the burning process (see Figure 6.15).
6. When the CD is finished being burned there will be an announcement by iTunes. Your audio CD is now ready for playing.

7

Creating or Obtaining Audio

Audio is one of the dimensions of a booktalk, which in many cases is a form of digital storytelling. The audio that you use in your booktalk most likely falls into one of three different categories: narration, background sounds, and soundtrack. Each of these categories can add depth to the booktalk being created.

NARRATION

Adding your own voice to a recorded booktalk adds depth to the presentation. Your speech, its rhythm, and your tone all provide insight into the story that you are presenting and help set up the interaction between the presenter and the story. Make sure that when you are narrating a booktalk, it doesn't sound like you are reading from a script. Yes, you may actually be reading from a script, but it shouldn't sound that way. Make sure that you have practiced what you will say and that you are comfortable and familiar with the content. Also, don't be afraid to ad-lib. One easy way to improve recording your own voice narration is to keep the writing short and then be prepared to record several takes. Being able to re-record is one of the nice things about using technology. If you don't like the sound of the first recording, then re-record the narration. Also, all too often people recording themselves talk too fast; slow down your speaking rate to make it easier for others to understand. Narration will require a microphone connected to your recording source.

BACKGROUND SOUND OR SOUND EFFECTS

Background sound, sound effects, or ambient sound can add complexity to your booktalk. These sounds can put the story into a real setting, add humor, or help focus the story. Think about a scary story where the narrator is describing a door opening. Now imagine that same story with the sound of a creaking door slowly opening—isn't that better? The use of sound effects can add a sense of realism to the booktalk. Experiment with different kinds of sound effects, but make sure that they become an enhancement to the booktalk. Don't let them become a distraction. Ambient sound puts the story into a location through sound. For example, if your booktalk was about Lemony Snicket's *The End*, then the sounds found at the beach would be good for the ambient sound. You could add the sound of the wind, the sound from the waves on the ocean,

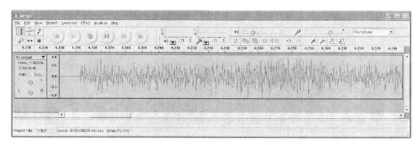

Figure 7.1. Author recording of ambient sound of the beach and seagulls.

and maybe the sounds from seagulls (see Figure 7.1). The ambient sound isn't the focus; instead it is the frame or the background that heightens the effect of the booktalk.

The following is a list of some of the available sites that provide sound resources online:

- **Ljudo:** http://ljudo.com
- **The Recordist:** http://www.therecordist.com/pages/downloads.html
- **Amazing Sounds:** http://amazingsounds.iespana.es/en
- **Simply the Best Sounds:** http://simplythebest.net/sounds/WAV/sound_effects_WAV/index.html
- **Wav Central:** http://www.wavcentral.com
- **Freesound:** http://freesound.iua.upf.edu

If a team of students is working on a technology-enhanced booktalk, one or more of them might want to assume the role of a Foley artist and create the background sound for the talk. Named after early practitioner Jack Foley, Foley artists are the people who create the sound effects for movies, television, and radio. Students can use the computer, sound recording software, and the microphone to create their own sounds to be added to the booktalk. Other times, students may want to go to a remote location and record the ambient sounds that are found there. For example, if some of the story is taking place during a football game, students could take a portable recorder and record the sound at the game to include in the booktalk.

SOUNDTRACK AND MUSIC

Today, people are used to encountering visual media in the context of music. Notice how many people use iPods, adding a soundtrack to their lives. A soundtrack helps set the mood of the presentation. Add background music that plays during your booktalk to enhance and reflect the story. Use sweet melodies for romances, upbeat tempos for happy endings, slow music for sadness, and fast music for action. No matter the type of music, rock, instrumental, jazz, or electronica, make sure that the music supports the booktalk by being appropriate to the story and not overwhelming the narration. For your soundtrack you can either use music that is already created, or create your own. If you want to use existing music, look online at some of the numerous sites that have published copyright-free music collections. Also, think about creating your own sound or customizing sounds that you find. Depending on your projects, you might need to have music or sound effects. There are a number of resources online that provide free audio files, often with no copyright restrictions. The following is a selection of some of the available sites that release music and sound:

- **Public Domain Audio:** http://pod safeaudio.com
- **Free Kids Music:** http://freekids music.com/music.html
- **FreePlayMusic:** http://freeplaymu sic.com
- **ccMixter:** http://ccmixter.org
- **SectionZ:** http://www.sectionz.com/cc.asp
- **DMusic:** http://www.dmusic.com
- **OpSound:** http://www.opsound.org
- **SoundClick:** http://www.sound click.com
- **MusOpen:** http://www.musopen.com
- **Jamendo:** http://www.jamendo.com/en

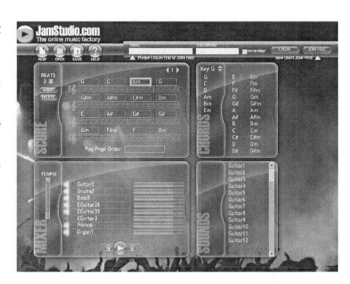

Figure 7.2. JamStudio online music creation tool. JamStudio.com screenshot used with permission of Chord Studio, Inc. Copyright © 2007 Chord Studio, Inc. All Rights Reserved.

Don't feel that you are limited to what others have created. Using the computer, microphone, and recording software you can record yourself or students playing their own music. If you don't have or play an instrument, there are a number of programs and online sites that let you even create your own music. For example, the site JamStudio (http://www.jamstudio.com; see Figure 7.2) allows users to create their own music directly online and gives you options of using guitar, drum, bass, and piano loops. Similar functions are part of other programs, such as Apple's GarageBand.

MICROPHONES

For many projects, such as podcasting or adding narration, you will need a microphone connected to a computer. While some computers have a microphone built in, they are often not acceptable for creating the audio for the booktalking projects. Issues with built-in and stick microphones can be caused by the user being too far from the microphone or users changing distances between themselves and the microphone. Because of these issues, we suggest obtaining a headset microphone for better quality recording. By wearing the microphone, the user has a consistent distance between the mouth and the microphone, and often this kind of microphone will pick up less room noise. The best choice for a microphone is one that plugs into the USB port. This way, the audio signal bypasses the sound card. If you don't have a headset microphone or USB connection, don't let it stop you or your students from getting started. Use what is available.

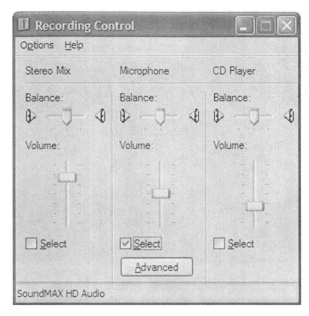

Figure 7.3. Setting the microphone as the audio source in Windows.

Select a Source

To record sound, you will need to make sure that the device with which you are recording is selected as the system's choice. To find out what your system is using as the recording source follow this path:

Start > Programs > Accessories > Entertainment > Volume Control (or double click on the speaker symbol by the clock in the lower right corner).

These steps will bring up the *Master Volume* window. To use the recording window, select **Options,** then **Properties,** and then select the **Recording** option. At the bottom of each input device will be a check box for either *Mute* or *Select.* Use the Mutes to avoid devices as sources, or use the Select to choose your audio source.

Depending on the microphone that you are using, it might need a little boost to get louder. This is necessary for microphones that do not have their own power source. If this is the case, click on the **Advanced** button below the microphone in the *Recording Control* panel (see Figure 7.3). In the *Advanced Controls for Microphone* select the option under *Other Controls* to turn on the **Microphone Boost.** Then click on the **Close** button.

Positioning Your Microphone Correctly

It is important to position a microphone so that when speaking, the air coming out of the speaker's mouth doesn't impact the surface of the microphone. If it does, then you will record loud popping noises during speech. One way to avoid this effect is the use of a wind screen that is positioned in front of the microphone. Another way is microphone placement. When wearing a headset microphone, try positioning the microphone slightly to the side of the mouth so it is not directly in front of your mouth. A good "rule of thumb" to follow on microphone positioning is to place the microphone a thumb-width from the edge of the mouth and a thumb thickness off the face (see Figure 7.4). Experiment with moving the microphone a little closer to or further from your mouth. Be careful so that extra sounds such as

Figure 7.4. Effective headset microphone positioning.

breathing or lip scraping are not inserted into your recording.

You can use a similar approach with a stick microphone. Find a comfortable position and then don't speak directly toward the microphone, but instead slightly to the side.

Quality Recording or Multiple People

For a high-quality recording, it is effective to use a good quality microphone. One that is easy to use and has USB connection is Blue Microphone's Snowball (http://www.bluemic.com; see Figure 7.5). The Snowball is a very good quality desktop microphone for recording spoken audio at a reasonable price ($100–$150). The Snowball microphone is a direct plug and play microphone that can connect to either a Mac or PC and needs no additional software. The Snowball can handle everything from individual soft vocals to student groups as you record your audio podcasts. Another relatively inexpensive quality USB microphone set is Podcast Factory from M-Audio (http://www.m-audio.com). For recording larger groups, a 360° or omnidirectional microphone may be needed.

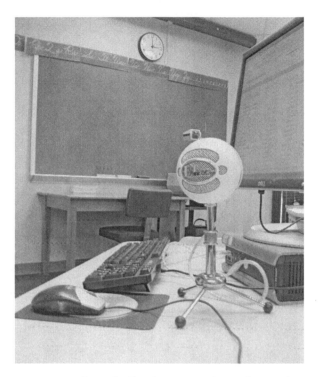

Figure 7.5. Snowball USB microphone from Blue Microphones.

8

Video Booktalks

Today it seems that digital video is king. In December of 2006, this was pointed out by *Time* Magazine when they chose "You" as the Person of the Year for 2006, as in YouTube and other Web 2.0 applications. According to *Time*, everyone participates in the creation of media: "for founding and framing the new digital democracy, for working for nothing and beating the pros at their own game, TIME's Person of the Year for 2006 is you" (Grossman, 2006). Not only are most students carrying cell phones, but these cell phones also are still and video cameras. It seems as if you can't find groups skateboarding anymore without one of them pulling out a camera or cell phone to film the others. In the educational setting, the structured use of digital video can positively impact the learning experience of both students and teachers, and activities that involve using or developing video can be particularly effective, especially when combined with other strategies such as problem-based and collaborative learning.

IN THE CLASSROOM

Groups Creating Video

Ms. Beck is a language arts and reading instructor in a middle school. She was nearly finished with her unit on the book *Old Yeller*. Throughout the unit the students had been reading the book and then participating cooperatively though literature circles activities. She knows from her polling of the class at the beginning of the unit that most of the students had never read the book and didn't exhibit much interest at the start, but by the end of the book the students were very involved and interested in the book itself and its topic. Also from listening to her students talk, she has heard a lot about YouTube and what the students have been watching. So her plan then is to have the students make their own video book commercials for the culminating event for the unit. These commercials will be used next year to help interest the next set of students in the readings and will also be posted to the YouTube site. The plan is to have the students continue to work in their literature circle groups and make their own YouTube video commercial for the book.

Before starting the video project, the teacher contacts the school's business and technology teacher and the school library media specialist, who assist her in the planning and obtaining the necessary resources for the project. Together they develop a set of resources that includes two scanners, a digital video camera, and six digital still

Figure 8.1. Ms. Beck's classroom setup.

cameras. To supplement Ms. Beck's four student computers, she borrows two more computers from other teachers in her house team and arranges to have them set up in her room so that there will be a computer for each of the six discussion groups (see Figure 8.1). Working with the other teacher and library media specialist, instructions are developed for each of the items used. Ms. Beck also develops the rubric that she will use to assess the finished videos.

The students are shown sample booktalking videos from the YouTube site, and the students are challenged to create their own videos for their project. Use of each of the different technology tools is demonstrated, and the evaluative rubric is reviewed. Over the next week as part of their daily class work, the student groups cooperatively use the classroom computers to develop their booktalk projects, completing a storyboard, writing a narration script, and creating the images that they wish to use. In making their videos, some student groups plan to use elements from their previous literature circle activities, such as scanning visualization drawings from various reading assignments, and others plan to create new images with a digital still or video camera. To create their videos the students use the video-editing program iMovie, which came with the computers, to assemble and edit the components of their videos.

When all of the videos are completed, the class can hold a video premier event where all the videos are shown to the class. Guest observers are asked to rate the videos and then awards are presented to the best and most original. At the end of their project the students upload their created work to the YouTube site.

LESSON PLAN: BOOKTALKING WITH IMOVIE

Length of Lesson: 9 days—50-minute class periods

Material: computers, iMovie software, pencils, storyboard handout.

Purpose/Outcomes/Objectives:

Students will read and analyze a book of their own choice in consultation with the teacher.

To enable students to personally relate to the literature that is read, the students will use software to create digital videos in the form of a booktalk that will encourage others to read the same book.

Standards Addressed:

AASL:

> 3.1.4 Use technology and other information tools to organize and display knowledge and understanding in ways that others can view, use, and access.

> 3.3.4 Create products that apply to authentic real-world contexts.

> 4.1.8 Use creative and artistic formats to express personal learning.

> 4.2.4 Show an appreciation for literature by electing to read for pleasure and expressing an interest in various literary genres. (AASL, 2007)

English Language Arts

Writing:

- LA.8.3.1.1—generating ideas from multiple sources based upon teacher-directed topics and personal interests;

- LA.8.3.1.2—making a plan for writing that addresses purpose, audience, main idea, logical sequence, and time frame for completion;

- LA.8.3.5.1—prepare writing using technology in a format appropriate to audience;

- LA.8.3.5.3—share the writing with the intended audience.

Media Literacy:

- LA.8.6.3.2—demonstrate the ability to select and ethically use print and nonprint media appropriate for the purpose, occasion, and audience to develop into a formal presentation;

Technology:

- LA.8.6.4.1—use appropriate available technologies to enhance communication and achieve a purpose (e.g., video, digital technology); and

- LA.8.6.4.2—evaluate and apply digital tools to publications and presentations.

Technology Standards

Students will design, develop, publish, and present products using technology resources that demonstrate and communicate curriculum concepts to audiences inside and outside the classroom (NETS Grades 6–8 performance indicator 6).

Beginning Stage

Once the student has finished reading the book, they will be asked to write a short summary about the book highlighting their favorite parts. They can include quotations from the book and any other information that they feel would help make a good booktalk.

Middle Stage

Students will be instructed on creating a storyboard. The library media specialist will model booktalking and explain how to construct the storyboard. The storyboard should act as a rough draft of the booktalk. The students should choose scenes or "hooks" that they plan to use in their iMovie presentation. Students will be instructed to discuss what scenes are the most important and use them in their presentation.

End Stage

Students will begin creating and editing their iMovie projects. The movie can highlight students giving their booktalks in front of the camera. For extra interest, students can act out selected scenes to go with their booktalk. This stage should take 3–5 days. Once students have finished editing, they will be able to create a DVD of their movie to share with the class.

Assessment: Booktalk iMovie

CATEGORY	4	3	2	1
Point of View—Awareness of Audience	Strong awareness of audience in the design. Students can clearly explain why they felt the vocabulary, audio, and graphics chosen fit the target audience.	Some awareness of audience in the design. Students can partially explain why they felt the vocabulary, audio, and graphics chosen fit the target audience.	Some awareness of audience in the design. Students find it difficult to explain how the vocabulary, audio, and graphics chosen fit the target audience.	Limited awareness of the needs and interests of the target audience.
Point of View—Purpose	Establishes a purpose early on and maintains a clear focus throughout.	Establishes a purpose early on and maintains focus for most of the presentation.	There are a few lapses in focus, but the purpose is fairly clear.	It is difficult to figure out the purpose of the presentation.
Images	Images create a distinct atmosphere or tone that matches different parts of the story. The images may communicate symbolism and/or metaphors.	Images create an atmosphere or tone that matches some parts of the story. The images may communicate symbolism and/or metaphors.	An attempt was made to use images to create an atmosphere/tone, but it needed more work. Image choice is logical.	Little or no attempt to use images to create an appropriate atmosphere/tone.
Soundtrack—Emotion	Music stirs a rich emotional response that matches the story line well.	Music stirs a rich emotional response that somewhat matches the story line.	Music is ok, and not distracting, but it does not add much to the story.	Music is distracting, inappropriate, OR was not used.
Details	The booktalk is given with exactly the right amount of detail throughout. It does not seem too short nor does it seem too long.	The booktalk is typically good, though it seems to drag somewhat OR needs slightly more detail in one or two sections.	The booktalk seems to need more editing. It is noticeably too long or too short in more than one section.	The booktalk needs extensive editing. It is too long or too short to be interesting. Too much information is revealed.
Length of Presentation	Length of presentation was between 2 and 5 minutes long.	Length of presentation was less than 2 minutes or longer than 5 minutes.	Length of presentation was longer than 5 minutes.	Presentation was less than 1 minute.

From *Tech-Savvy Booktalkers: A Guide for 21st-Century Educators* by Nancy J. Keane and Terence W. Cavanaugh. Westport, CT: Libraries Unlimited. Copyright © 2009.

ONLINE VIDEO BOOKTALKS

There are already a good number of video booktalks available on the Web from a variety of sources. Many students, teachers, library media specialists, librarians, and others have created video booktalks that can be downloaded or played online. Some of the booktalk sites offer digital videos of a person reading from or talking about a book, and this type of video resembles a news anchor. For example, Prairie Middle School's Web site has a set of videos showing their students talking about books (see Figure 8.2).

Other organizations go much further in developing booktalks to the point of creating whole new movies and placing them online. For example, the Digital Booktalks site at the University of Central Florida creates film features with sets, actors, and special effects. To direct students to these sites, teachers or library media specialists can set up class or school Web pages with links for easy connection. Teachers can use the sites as introductions to books that the students may be reading in class.

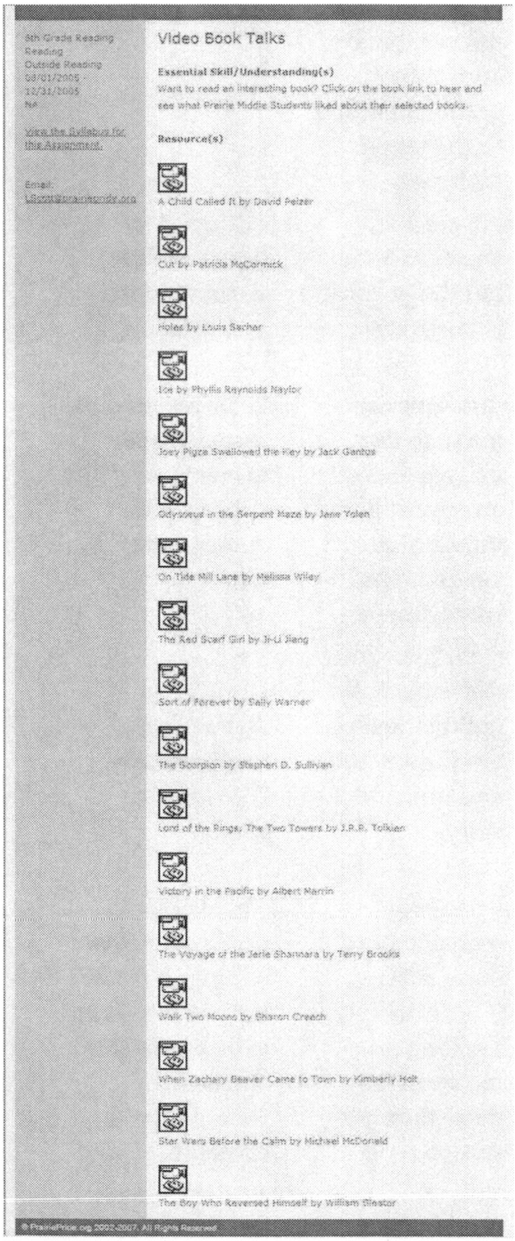

Sample Online Video Booktalk Sites

Apple Education Language Arts (look at Short Story Commercials and Book Ads): http://education.apple.com/education/ilife/subject_template.php?subject_id=2
Bookwink: http://bookwink.com
Digital Booktalks©: http://www.digitalbooktalk.com
Prairie Middle Students Video Book Talks: http//www.prairiepride.org/teachertools/ViewAssignment.php?AssignID=19589&SylID=327
Teachers@Random: http://www.randomhouse.com/teachers/librarians/booktalks.html

CREATING A VIDEO BOOKTALK FROM STILL IMAGES

With digital technologies and programs such as iMovie, Movie Maker, and PhotoStory, video booktalks are relatively easy to create using still images. Using these programs and still images can save a lot of time, effort, and expense because no video cameras are needed, and there is no learning curve or software needed to edit video. Teachers and school

Figure 8.2. Student Video Book Talks from Prairie Middle School's Web site, presenting video booktalks in QuickTime format (http://www.prairiepride.org/teachertools/ViewAssignment.php?AssignID=19589&SylID=327).

media personnel can quickly create their own video booktalks from stills to share. Even better, students can create video booktalks as a class project. Educator- and student-created video booktalks can be placed on a CD or uploaded to the school Web site for school and home use. Student-created video booktalks make an excellent technology integration activity that meets two of the ISTE (2000) National Educational Technology Standards for Students concerning technology use for personal productivity and as communication tools because the students use the technology to produce and share their creative works.

The person doing the booktalk, whether it is the teacher, library media specialist, or student, should write out a draft of the talk to refer to as narration. This narrative script may include a description of the book, such as those found on the back covers or in an online bookstore. The next step is to start finding or making pictures to include with the talk. You will need to find or create some pictures for the project that help portray the story's elements or characters. Book cover images can be taken with a digital camera, scanner, or found on the publisher's Web site or Amazon.com. Other pictures can be found from image databases on the Internet, such as from Flickr (http://www.flickr.com/creativecommons), a free resource of noncopyrighted images. Multimedia search engines, such as Google (http://images.google.com), can be used to search for appropriate images. Pictures can also be drawn using computer programs or drawn on paper and then scanned or digitally photographed. It is usually better when searching to find more items than will actually be used rather than too few. The pictures should be saved on a computer to a single location or removable medium, such as a flash drive, making it easier to find them later when using the video creation program. Depending on your computer system and the software you will use, you might find or create other forms of media including audio and video.

Consider using aids as you start your project. Planning tools such as storyboards can save a lot of time, and they provide activities students can do when computers are unavailable. (For more information on storyboards see Chapter 4.)

Depending on the available computers and the operating system that they are running, there are free programs that can be used to create video booktalks. The following free video production software programs do not require a video camera or finding or converting video recordings in order to make video booktalks. These programs can create the video from stills, using digital photographs, drawings, and sound files (Table 8.1). To record the booktalk narration, a microphone connected to a computer is needed. These software programs will turn the images and sounds into a video file from project file. The video files can be watched using players such as QuickTime and Windows Media Player.

Table 8.1
Video creation programs

Program	Extension	Platform
Movie Maker	.wmv	Windows
PhotoStory	.wmv	Windows
iMovie	.mov	Macintosh

CREATING VIDEO BOOKTALKS USING MICROSOFT PHOTOSTORY

Microsoft's PhotoStory is a very user-friendly program that is available from the Microsoft Web site at no charge. It will run on a Windows XP computer and is very

useful for creating multimedia booktalks. Using a five-step process, the program creates video without the use of a video camera or video recordings. Instead, PhotoStory makes the video from stills, using digital photographs, drawings, and sound files. To record your narration you will need to connect a microphone to your computer. The software will process the images and sounds into a video at the end. The final video files (.wmv) can be played using Windows Media Player 7 or later (see Figure 8.3) or with other programs that will play .wmv files, such as Real Player and Quick-

Figure 8.3. Video booktalk being played with Windows Media Player.

Time (with the wmv plugin). The files can also be converted into another format, such as flash, using additional software.

You will need to download and install Microsoft PhotoStory from the Web site (http://www.microsoft.com/photostory). After installation, start the PhotoStory program and select the option to create a new project. Create your booktalk video using

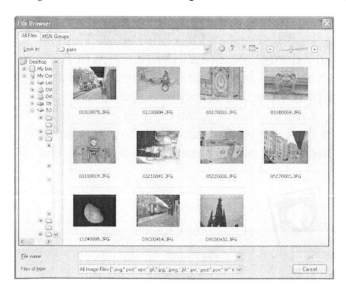

the PhotoStory program's five-step process. Before you begin recording your booktalk, you should first write a script, an outline or a storyboard, and then plan the pictures that correspond with each part of your script (see Chapter 4 for more information on storyboarding).

Step 1: Import and Arrange Your Pictures

Import your pictures from the folder into the PhotoStory project by clicking on the **Import Pictures...** button. Browse to the folder where you have saved your images. You can select multiple images by holding down the **Ctrl** key as you click with your mouse on the icon. Once all the

Figure 8.4. Importing images into the PhotoStory booktalk project.

images you wish to use have been selected, click the **OK** button to bring the images into the project (see Figure 8.4).

You should also arrange the pictures in the order that you want them to appear in the final video by dragging the image thumbnails and rearranging them in the sequence that is desired (see Figure 8.5). There are image tools that will allow you to adjust the color, rotate the image, and do basic image editing. You can also change the picture by selecting from the **Edit** and then **Add Effect** menu.

Once you have your pictures arranged the way you want them, click on the **Save Project...**button, and then click on the **Next** button.

Step 2: Add Titles to Your Pictures

Once you have your pictures inserted in the project, you can add titles over the pictures (see Figure 8.6). Type in the text you want on the screen in the text box. The titles can be placed in different locations on the screen using the menu buttons. You can also change the color, font size, and font type by clicking on the select font button. Click on different pictures to add titles to them.

Once you have created all of the titles, click on the **Save Project...**button, and then click on the **Next** button.

Figure 8.5. The picture adjustment and arrangement frame in Microsoft's Photo Story.

Figure 8.6. Adding title overlays to pictures in Photo Story.

Step 3: Narrate Your Pictures and Customize Motion

In this step you can add your own audio track and decide how you want your pictures to move and change. Each picture has its own audio recording and individual movement.

Movement

By default each picture is displayed for five seconds before changing to the next. You can change this amount for any picture by clicking on the **Customize Motion...**button. You can also use this option to change the way the picture is displayed. Here you can adjust the portion of the image to display at the start and at the end of the time during which the picture is displayed. The computer will then create a motion effect

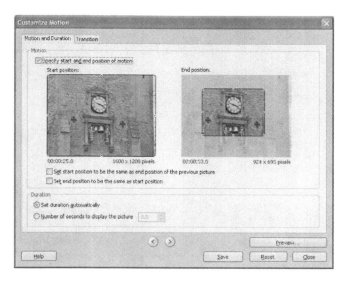

Figure 8.7. Setting the motion of the screen action in PhotoStory.

between the two settings. For example, you can begin with a wide view of the picture and then zoom into a section of the image (see Figure 8.7). To change the size or position of motion, first click in the box to **Specify start and end position of motion,** then click on either the left or right image. Adjust the size by clicking and dragging the corner boxes to show the portion you want displayed. Adjust the position by clicking and dragging the image box to the desired location. Viewers will see a smooth zooming transition from the wide angle to the small focus. Select each picture and change the motion or duration as desired. The second tab here allows the user to change the transition effect between pictures. The default is a cross fade, but each picture can have its own transition from the 50 available options. Click on the arrows near the bottom of the window to change between pictures. Once you have your motions and transitions set, click the **Close** button to return to the project window. Click on the **Save Project...** button.

Audio Narration

An effective strategy for recording your script is to either type in or copy from a document the text that you want to read into the notes space provided. Alternately, you can use a storyboard sheet with your own script. When speaking into a microphone, it works better not to speak directly into it but instead across it (this avoids the popping noise of air hitting the microphone). The best kind of microphone in this case is one that is

Figure 8.8. Adding audio narration to the PhotoStory project.

worn, such as a head microphone. Place the microphone so that it is a thumb width to the side of the mouth. When you are ready to record, click on the picture to which you want to add your narration and then click on the **record** button (see Figure 8.8). When you have finished adding the narration for that image, click on the **stop** button. If you make any mistakes, you can click the **Delete narration** button and start again for this image. The display time will adjust to your recording time, so you will not need to go back to the **Customize Motion** section to change the amount of time for the image. Click on a different thumbnail picture or use the arrows under the large picture to change to another image and add a new narration.

Once you have the movements, transitions, and narrations set, save your project, and then click on the **Next** button.

Step 4: Add Background Music

You can next add background music that plays during your story by either selecting from music saved on your computer or by creating new music within the PhotoStory software (see Figure 8.9). Similar to the movements, transitions, and narrations, it is possible for a different piece of music to play for each picture or for a group of pictures. Click on the **Select Music** button to choose a piece of music saved as a digital file from your computer, a network folder, or the Internet. Clicking on the **Create Music** button allows you to adjust or customize specialized prerecorded music by selecting the genre, style, bands, mood, tempo, and intensity of the music. We prefer the Create Music option, which allows the music to be more tailored to the booktalk. In addition, the built-in music is not copyright protected, so you can safely exhibit or Web-publish the completed booktalks. Click on the first picture of the project, and then click on the music button. Try playing with the options, making adjustments until you have the background that you feel goes with your book, and then click the **OK** button (see Figure 8.10). The music will now spread across the entire project. You should adjust the volume setting of the background music. We suggest that you set the volume at half or lower so that it doesn't interfere with the narration. If you wish, you can click on another picture and set the music for that one.

Click on the **Preview** button to preview the look and sound of your movie.

Once you have the background music set, save your project and then click on the **Next** button.

Figure 8.9. Adding background music to the Photo Story project.

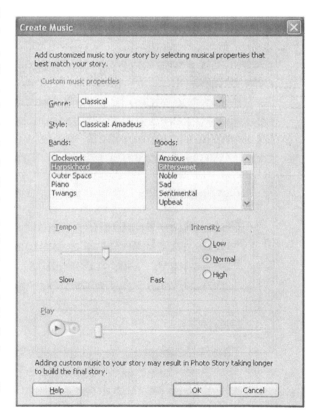

Figure 8.10. Creating background music by selecting genre, style, mood, tempo, and so forth in PhotoStory.

Step 5: Save Your Story

It is now time to save your project as a movie file (*.wmv). At this stage the program will take the project file (*.wp3) and create a separate movie file. While PhotoStory gives you a variety of options, you can use the **Save your story for playback on your computer** (see Figure 8.11). You will need to go into the **Settings...** to select one of the

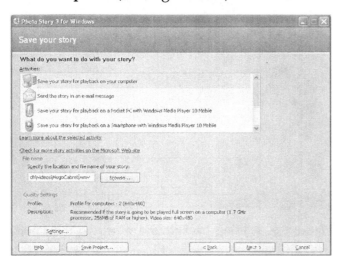

built in options. We suggest that you pick from the Profiles 1–4 for computers, understanding that the larger screen setting will cause the movie to have a larger file size. If you are planning to create a Video CD or DVD and play your booktalks on a television, you should choose those options. You will then need to import the movie into a DVD/CD Video creation program to actually burn the movie onto a disc. The smallest file size would be the one for e-mail, but this one would also have the least clarity when viewed on a screen.

Figure 8.11. Selecting the file setting and location of the created video file from PhotoStory.

Click on the **Next** button now to start the building process, during which the program converts your project into a movie file. Once this building process is completed, the program will offer the option of watching your finished video or starting a new project.

A sample video booktalk that is 3 minutes long, with 11 images, music, and narration, and saved for a 640 x 480 pixel display, took up only 3.45 Megabytes of space. (A sample video booktalk made with PhotoStory 3 is available for download from http://www.drscavanaugh.org/ebooks/pendragon.wmv.)

Resource Sites

PhotoStory Booktalking: http://www.drscavanaugh.org/ebooks/booktalk.htm
Microsoft PhotoStory download: http://www.microsoft.com/photostory
PhotoStory Tutorials: http://www.microsoft.com/windowsxp/using/digital
   photography/photostory/tips/firststory.mspx

IMOVIE

The iMovie program is usually bundled in most Apple computers and is also available for download from the Apple Web site. The downloaded program will run on a computer with an operating system of Mac OS X v10.3.4 or later and will make videos that will play with the QuickTime 6.5.2 player and later. To make your video from the stills, you will first need your pictures imported into the program. Once the images have been added to the storyboard at the bottom of the window, you can select to also use the Ken Burns Effect to give still pictures motion. Switch to the **Audio** section to add your narration. Record your narration into the program by clicking on the first thumbnail image and then pressing the **record** button. Press the **record** button again to stop recording. If you have recorded music files on your computer, you can add them to the other audio track in the story board. Be sure to check the adjust volume box and decrease the volume of the music track so that it doesn't interfere with the narration. You can change the display length of the book cover pictures to better match the narration by switching back to the **Photo** section and sliding the timing bar. Add text to the pictures as in the **Titles** button and then fill in the text boxes and select the movement; click the **Update** button to lock in the titles (see Figure 8.12). Transitions between pictures can be added by dragging and dropping from the **Trans** collection and placing them between the thumbnail images in the storyboard. The iMovie program can

Figure 8.12. Adding text over pictures to a video booktalk project using iMovie.

also add video effects to the movie such as aging the film or changing it to black and white. Once the booktalk project is complete, use the **Export** option in the **File** menu to make a QuickTime video from the iMovie project.

Booktalk using iMovie: http://www.users.ties.k12.mn.us/~wbierden/booktalk.htm

Apple iMovie download: http://www.apple.com/ilife/imovie

iMovie program tutorials: http://www.apple.com/support/imovie

MAKING VIDEO MORE INTERESTING

When creating or recording video for a booktalk, there are basically two kinds of tools to use to create the video: a self-contained digital video camera or a camera directly connected to a computer, such as a webcam.

A digital video camera records the video direct to computer-useable video format without needing to capture the video again, which you would have to do if you used a VHS video camera. There are numerous models of digital video cameras (also known as camcorders) sold today from well-known manufacturers such as Sony, Panasonic, JVC, and Canon, and they can record onto digital tape, discs, or even to their own hard drives. These cameras usually have a USB or FireWire port so that you can download the video onto your computer quickly and easily.

A webcam or Internet camera is a form of video camera that must be directly connected to a computer to work. While often used to share images, such as using online meeting software, these cameras can also be used to record video for other purposes. Using computer software, the user captures the video from the camera into the computer. The capture process will usually create .AVI (on the PC) or .MOV (on the Apple) files on your computer's hard disk. These files contain your video, frame by frame, often in the maximum resolution that your camera can produce, which means large files. Files sizes may run as large as 1 gigabyte for 3 minutes of video or 10 gigabytes for 30 minutes of video.

Before you purchase any video camera for your booktalks, first check to see what is already available, perhaps in the library or through the schools' technology coordinator. Also remember to check the digital still camera that may be available because many still digital cameras can also record video that may be usable for your booktalk. It may even be possible to use your cell phone to record your video.

If you need to purchase a video recording tool, check on whether one of the less expensive ones will be sufficient for your school. For less than $100 it is possible to get a relatively good video camera for your computer, either a webcam or a small handheld digital video camera.

Webcams come in a variety of styles, some that sit by themselves, others that attach to a laptop's screen, and some are built in to a laptop. Visit a local electronics store to find a number of these cameras. Review their features and decide which you would prefer to have. You may need to run the camera's software to record your video, or you may be able to use video-editing software such as Windows Movie Maker or Apple iMovie to capture your video.

If you want more mobility than a tethered webcam can offer, then you will need a digital video camera. There are a number of inexpensive digital video cameras: RCA's Small Wonder or the Flip Video camera are just two that work well for recording video booktalks. These cameras usually come in various recording capacities, such as 30 or 60 minutes. Look for a camera, such as the Flip Video camera, that uses nonproprietary AA batteries for power. The Flip Video records approximately two hours with just two standard AA batteries and up to five hours when using the lithium AA batteries. These cameras usually store the video as standard .AVI files, and can work with either the Mac or PC. When connected to the computer, the camera shows up as an additional hard drive that you can explore.

We suggest that you look for a video camera that has the tripod mount on the bottom. This way you will be able to place your camera on any standard tripod or other camera mount for your video recording.

MAKING BETTER VIDEO

There are a few things that you can do to make your videos look much better, including positioning the camera, setting the shot, and considering time. These things are not hard to do, but it is surprising how much of a difference that they can make.

Position the Camera

When you shoot video in a single location, you should use a tripod or other camera stabilization device. Video does not look good with a shaking image. Tripods come in all sizes and quality; there are even acceptable ones at a dollar store. You should only move your camcorder when necessary. Typically, when recording a person giving a booktalk, you will shoot close shots. If you are filming yourself or someone else talking, then you should be within 6 feet (2 meters) of the camera. Keep your video simple and uncomplicated, without much happening in the video and movement kept to a minimum.

Setting

Consider where you will record your video. Make sure there is enough light and that the light is in front of the person on camera rather than behind them. Backlighting a person puts the face in shadows. For indoor recording, use a directional light if possible. Set the camera's white balance at every location (if this feature is available).

Video usually includes background elements in the location where it is shot. Make sure what's in the background of your video doesn't draw your viewer's attention from your main subject. Avoid locations where the background may always have movement, such as by a window where people may be walking past.

Figure 8.13. Rule of thirds applied to a close picture.

Composing the Shot or the Rule of Thirds

People often record video with the on-camera person right in the middle of the screen, which makes the scene less interesting. This technique is called headhunting. Instead, shift the camera so that the subject is a little to the side from the center to make the video more interesting. Good shot composition uses the "Rule of Thirds" for positioning of the person on camera. To use the rule of thirds, you treat the camera's screen as being divided into a tic-tac-toe pattern. When you shoot your video, place your subject along those imaginary lines. When you are framing the person on camera, adjust the camera so that the person falls along one of the third lines, preferably with elements of the face at a point where those lines intersect.

When shooting close to a person, frame the face so that the eyes are on the top line and the center of the head is on the left or the right line (see Figure 8.13). While this method may seem strange at first, it provides the proper balance and helps to make your shot more professional.

If you are shooting from a bit farther back then place the subject along a whole line, either the left or right line (see Figure 8.14). This will have the person noticeably

Figure 8.14. Rule of thirds being applied to a full-person shot.

off from the center and therefore creating an additional point of interest to his/her side, a good place to put the book being discussed.

10-Second Rule

When recording, start about 10 seconds before the action in your scene actually begins, in this case the action is the booktalking. Continue recording for about 10 seconds after action has ended. Recording these extra seconds is very helpful when you transfer your video recording to the editing software.

To make a more professional video, shoot from a variety of angles. For example, if you are shooting with a single camera, stop occasionally to change person/camera placement. These edits can then be "spliced" back together using the editing software to make the complete video.

If you watch a TV show and pay attention to the filming, you should notice how rare it is for the camera angle to remain the same for more than 10 or 15 seconds. To help keep the video interesting, a director "cuts" or changes between different viewing angles. For example, the screen might show a student's face while he's talking for five seconds, before switching to a shot of the book cover. Keep your shot steady for at least 10 seconds before panning (moving the camera left or right) or zooming (getting closer or further away).

LESSON PLAN: RECORDING VIDEO BOOKTALKS

Purpose/Outcomes/Objectives:

The purpose of this lesson is to practice public speaking and persuasion. Students will be videotaped presenting a booktalk for a favorite book. The booktalk will be videotaped by another student. Students will use video-editing software to edit the booktalk. Students will work in teams on the editing of the video. The teams will create a group video of all the booktalks from the team. The overall goal of the booktalk is to persuade the audience to read the book. The final projects will be posted for the entire class to share.

Description:

Students will work with the library media specialist to complete this project. Students will work individually to storyboard and draft the script for the booktalk. The student will practice before taping. Students will use a video camera to tape booktalks and import video clips into video-editing software. Once the individual scripts have been taped, students will work in groups to sequence movie clips, add title screens for definition of genre and title/author lists, and add transitions between clips.

Standards Addressed:

AASL

2.2.4 Demonstrate personal productivity by completing products to express learning.

3.1.4 Use technology and other information tools to organize and display knowledge and understanding in ways that others can view, use, and assess.

4.1.3 Respond to literature and creative expressions of ideas in various formats and genres. (AASL, 2007).

ISTE Technology Foundation Standards for Students

(3.1) Students use technology tools to enhance learning, increase productivity, and promote creativity.

(4.1) Students use telecommunications to collaborate, publish, and interact.

(4.2) Students use a variety of media and formats to communicate information

Tasks:

Day 1: Pre-assessment: Students will determine which book to focus on. They will use journal writing to describe the book. The journal entries will be used to create the booktalk that will be videotaped. The teacher and the library media specialist will use the journal entry to determine teams. The teams may be based on genre, theme, author, or other criteria.

Day 2 and 3: Scripts: The students will be assigned to a team. In their team, they will use their journal writing as a springboard to creating a booktalk script. The teacher and the library media specialist provide a starter to include:

My favorite book is _____ by _____.
This book is about _____ (do not give away the ending).
You'll love this book if _____ "

The library media specialist will model booktalks from a variety of genres and booktalking styles. The teacher or school librarian may present a mini-lesson on writing three sentence summaries if needed. Students can create their own scripts as long as they include the necessary information.

The students will practice scripts with a partner in their team at least five times. The partner will give suggestions to improve presentation (volume, pausing, pacing, eye contact, articulation, etc.). The teacher or the school librarian working together can also model poor presentations and elicit suggestions from the whole class to model the types of suggestions they should offer to their partners. The school librarian should co-teach and model good presentations so that students will understand the expectations.

Day 4: Videography: The students will videotape presenting their scripts. Students may use simple props/costumes to bring the script to life. Minimally, the student should have a copy of the book for display in the presentation.

Day 5: Edit: Students will edit video clips. Students will include a title screen and a list of the book titles with authors. Students can add transitions if they have time. Students will assist one another to navigate the screens in the video-editing software. The teacher or library media specialist should give an orientation mini-lesson to help students with the different options and use of resources.

Rubric for Booktalk

	1	2	3
Has book in hand			
Includes title, author, and publication information			
Uses an introduction that grabs the audience's attention			
Maintains eye contact			
Uses information from the book (e.g. names of characters and places)			
Demonstrates enthusiasm for book			
Uses interesting passages from book			
Tells enough to gain interest but does not reveal the ending of the book			
Uses conclusion that makes us want to read the book			
Stays within time limits			
Overall presentation			
Comments:			

Rubric for Video Presentation

	1	2	3
Minimum of 1 minute booktalk			
Title, author, and publication information for the book			
Video is clear and audio can be heard			
Cover of the book			
Spelling and grammar			
Conveys the sense of the book			
Overall presentation			
Comments			

From *Tech-Savvy Booktalkers: A Guide for 21st-Century Educators* by Nancy J. Keane and Terence W. Cavanaugh. Westport, CT: Libraries Unlimited. Copyright © 2009.

Assessment:

The teacher will assess clear speaking skills and inclusion of the three elements: title and author (correct spelling), synopsis of plot, and why you'd love this book.

Students will self-assess by watching the videos and using the rubric for booktalks to determine areas of improvement. The students will use outcomes from rubrics to create a class criterion for future booktalk projects.

Technology Tools and Resources:

- Computers
- Video-editing software
- Digital video camcorder, tapes, firewire
- Simple props related to books
- Music for title screens (optional)

USING WINDOWS MOVIE MAKER TO CREATE BOOKTALK VIDEO

Windows Movie Maker is available for free download and is often already installed in computers running a Windows operating system. To create their video, users will need to first find or create and save images that they plan to use in their presentation. It is suggested that all resources the students will use in their booktalk project, such as videos, images, and audio files, should be stored in a single folder on the computer or attached storage drive. These files will be imported into the booktalking project using the Movie Maker program.

Using Movie Maker to create videos is a three-step process with a number of sub-steps in a drag and drop interface. First, bring your media into the project, then add the parts that you want to the timeline or storyboard along with other items such as text and transitions, and then finally save the project as a playable video file.

To create your booktalk video, start the Movie Maker program. If you do not have Movie Maker, it can be downloaded from: http://www.microsoft.com/moviemaker.

Once the program has started, select the option for a **New Project** from the **File** menu. (To achieve a higher level of control over the program, we suggest that you use the Timeline view instead of the Storyboard, and that you expand the video section of the timeline.)

Step 1: Capture Video

The first thing to know is that the Capture Video section is not limited to capturing video but is actually used for assembling the materials or contents for your video. In this section, you can drop in any mixture of audio files, images, and video files. The Windows Movie Maker program can import any of the following file types into a video project:

- Audio files: .aif, .aifc, .aiff .asf, .au, .mp2, .mp3, .mpa, .snd, .wav, and .wma
- Picture files: .bmp, .dib, .emf, .gif, .jfif, .jpe, .jpeg, .jpg, .png, .tif, .tiff, and .wmf
- Video files: .asf, .avi, .m1v, .mp2, .mp2v, .mpe, .mpeg, .mpg, .mpv2, .wm, and .wmv

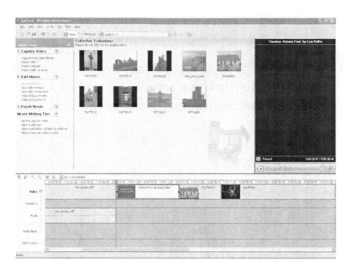

Figure 8.15. Microsoft Windows Movie Maker's Movie Tasks pane.

To import you media files, you can either use the *Movie Tasks of Import video, Import Picture and Import audio or music* (see Figure 8.15), or you can drag and drop the files from a folder into the *Collections* space. You can preview the images and clips by selecting them from the *Collections* list and viewing it in the *Monitor* pane.

The *Monitor* pane has additional functions beyond displaying the select image or playing the video in the timeline. If you import a video, you can use the *Monitor* to capture a picture from the video or to slice the video into smaller sections to use. Play with the two buttons on the bottom right of the preview pane to practice editing a video in the collection.

Once the *Collection* has all the elements that are planned for the project, drag the files from the *Collections* settings onto the *Timeline* (or Storyboard) section. Drag still images or video files onto the *Video* track and audio files onto the *Audio/Music* track. You can rearrange the video elements by dragging them into the order that you want. Change the length of time on an element by clicking on its edge and dragging it to be longer or shorter. Initially, all stills dragged to the *Timeline/Storyboard* are set for five seconds. Please note that you can change the display time for a still to either longer or shorter, but you can only shorten a video clip.

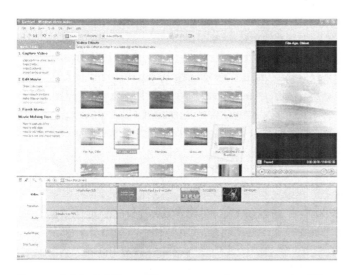

Figure 8.16. Adding effects to a video project in Windows Movie Maker.

Step 2: Edit Movie

With the elements of your booktalk video assembled as you want them in the *Timeline* or *Storyboard*, move to the second section and add edits or effects to make the movie more interesting (see Figure 8.16).

Using the *View video effects*, you can view a list of possible effects that can be added to your video. Some of the effects are changing the movie to making a clip look like an old movie to changing the color or rotating the image. Drag the video effect down and drop it on an item in the *Video* track of the timeline to give it that effect.

The *View video transitions* works much the same as the video effects, but the transitions change the way the picture changes as it moves from one image to the next. Drag and drop the transition between two images in the timeline to add the transition effect. The transition effect will cause the two clip elements to overlap, and a mark will be added to the *Transition* line. The transition mark can be time adjusted like an image by clicking on the edge and dragging it to be either longer or shorter. Be aware that changing the length of the transition effects the picture overlap: The longer the transition the larger the picture overlap. It may become necessary to expand the picture display time to make sure that the image is displayed long enough to be seen.

The *Make titles or credits* section allows you to add text to the video. Adding titles to the beginning, before, after, or at the end will create a new frame just for the text. Adding titles on a clip creates an overlay, showing both the text and the image underneath. The text information added to the video can be animated to change its appearance in the video, along with adjusting for the text's size, font, and color.

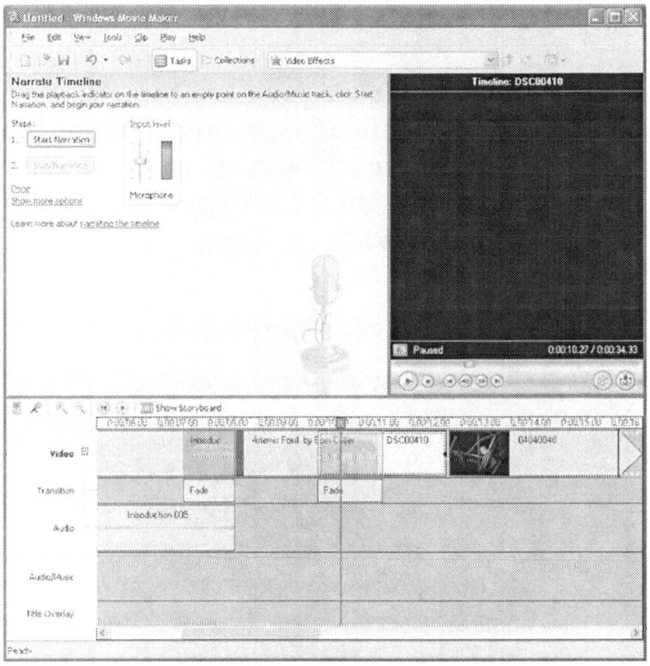

After the effects have been selected,

Figure 8.17. Adding narration to a video booktalk project using Windows Movie Maker.

the narration should be added. Move the playback mark on the timeline to where you would like the narration to begin and press the microphone button above the timeline or use the **Narrate timeline** option in the **Tools** menu (see Figure 8.17). This narration will become the Audio/Music track, so you will not be able to add additional music. Connect your microphone to your computer, select the **Start Narration** button and speak into your microphone to record. When you have finished with your narration for the booktalk, select the **Stop Narration** button to stop recording. The system will prompt you to save the narration track and then add it to your video. You should notice that the Audio/Music track indicates the narration with the name that you saved it under.

Step 3: Finish Movie

The last steps are to save the movie. Start by completing the **Properties** from the **File** menu, adding information such as the *Title, Author,* and *Description.* This is a good time to again save the project file, in case edits are needed later.

To save the booktalk video as a movie either select one of the options from *3. Finish Movie* task or select the **Save Movie File** option from the **File** menu. Where you will show your booktalk video may effect the format you use to save the movie. Initially, we suggest that you save to *My Computer* and use the default settings.

Select the **Next** button to save your movie to the selected location.

Resources

About.com—Desktop Video Tutorials for Windows Movie Maker: http://desktopvideo.about.com/od/moviemakertutorials/Windows_Movie_Maker_Tutorials_Learn_to_Edit_Video_With_Movie_Maker.htm

Microsoft Windows Movie Maker download: http://www.microsoft.com/movie maker

Movie Maker program tutorials: http://www.microsoft.com/windowsxp/using/ moviemaker/getstarted/default.mspx

University of Texas' Introduction to Windows Movie Maker: http://www.ischool. utexas.edu/technology/tutorials/graphics/moviemaker2

Windows Movie Maker Forums: http://www.windowsmoviemakers.net/Forums

Online Video Tools

The following are video tools that allow users to upload, edit, and remix video to create content, which is playable through a Web browser.

Eyespot—http://eyespot.com
JayCut—http://jaycut.com
Jumpcut—http://www.jumpcut.com
Motionbox—http://www.motionbox.com
Splashcast—http://web.splashcast.net
TouFee—http://www.toufee.com

POSTING TO YOUTUBE

Not only can library media specialists, teachers, and students make booktalking videos for their school, they can easily post a booktalk video to a social networking video site such as YouTube, TeacherTube, or GoogleVideo.

It is important to remind students that because these videos are being published and available for any Web user, copyright-friendly or creative commons images, sound, and video must be used for the content. The best case is to use tools to create original images, sound, and video.

Video booktalk creators may share additional aspects of their production, such as scripts, storyboards, and their created images as they develop their booktalk video.

How to Post to YouTube

Currently all videos uploaded to YouTube have a 100MB file size limit and a time limit of 10-minutes. Also, the finished booktalk video must be in one of the following formats for YouTube to accept the file: Windows Media (.wmv), QuickTime (.mov), MPEG (.mpg), or Audio-Video Interleaved (.avi).

1. Begin uploading your video by visiting the YouTube homepage (http:// www.youtube.com), and either create an account by selecting **Sign Up** or by logging in to an existing account using **Log In.** Next select the link that says **Upload Videos.**

2. You should now see the *Video Upload* page (see Figure 8.18), where you will complete the identification process of your video. Give your booktalk video a title, a description, keywords that you would expect people to use to find your video, and a category. You can set the *Broadcast Options* to be

either public or private. The *Date and Map Options* are used to indicate the date that the video was made and where it was made on a map. Alternately, use the map feature to indicate where the book's story takes place. The *Sharing Options* are used to allow watchers to respond, such as with ratings or comments. When this page is complete click on the **Upload a video...** button.

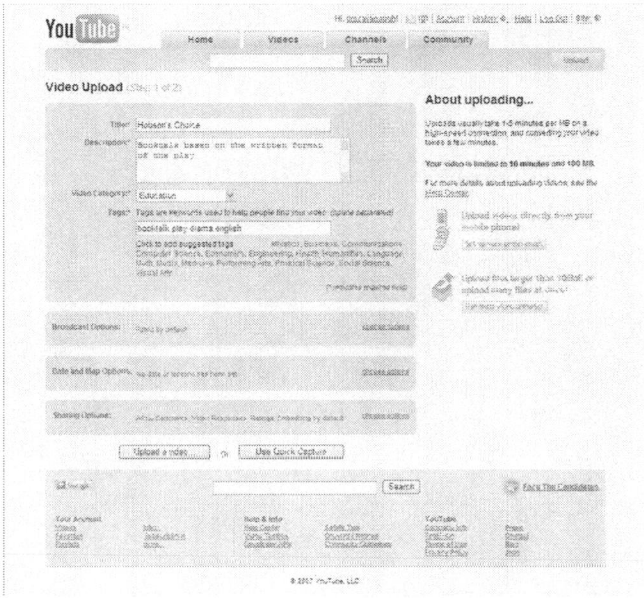

3. You should see the Video Upload page. Use the **Browse** button to access your computer and select the video to upload. Then select the **Upload Video** button to copy the video to the YouTube site.

Figure 8.18. YouTube's uploading video page. Copyright © Google 2007.

4. Once your video has finished uploading, it will be processed by YouTube so that it can be streamed from the site, so there will be a slight delay between posting your booktalk video and being able to watch it on the site. YouTube will provide the necessary HTML code that is used to embed your booktalk video on a Web site other than YouTube.

Uploading videos to either TeacherTube or Google Videos follows a similar process.

REFERENCES

American Association of School Librarians (AASL). (2007). AASL Standards for the 21st-Century Learner. Retrieved May 3, 2008, from http://www.ala.org/ala/aasl/aaslprof tools/learningstandards/AASL_Learning_Standards_2007.pdf.

Grossman, L. (2006, December 13). Time's Person of the Year: You. *Time Magazine*. Retrieved September, 2007, from http://www.time.com/time/magazine/article/0,9171,1569514,00.html.

ISTE. (2000). National Educational Technology Standards for Students. Retrieved August 1, 2007 from http://www.iste.org/Content/NavigationMenu/NETS/ForTeachers/2000stan dards/ NETS_for_Teachers2000.htm.

9

Booktalking Kiosks

By adapting existing computer equipment in schools, it is possible to create a video booktalk kiosk to advertise books using recorded booktalks. Near the entrance of stores you might notice a music or video kiosk or display that continually plays short segments of music and/or videos to entice the shopper to buy the product. Video rental stores use a looping commercial sequence played on the display screens to promote videos available for rent or sale. Depending on your booktalk file types, you can show your booktalks using presentation or video software. Using a program such as PowerPoint, a number of booktalk presentations can be inserted into a single presentation, and then set up to loop continuously. Using a computer's video player program, such as Windows Media Player, with downloaded or created booktalk videos, a teacher or school media specialist can set up a computer as a book advertising kiosk (see Figure 9.1). Additionally, the computer's video program can randomly play and repeat the videos throughout the day in the atrium of the library, the school office, or other location in the school, including the school's closed-circuit television system room.

Placing your booktalking kiosk in a well traveled or noticeable location, such as near the entrance to the library, is an effective way for getting book information to large numbers of students. Another popular location is where students wait or relax, but take care not to disturb those reading. If possible, set up your booktalking kiosk with a screen multiplier. That way a single computer can be used to play the booktalks on multiple screens. Set up one of the screens so that it can be seen from outside the library, such as the hallway.

KIOSK COMPONENTS

Computer

You do not need a very new or powerful computer for your booktalking kiosk. The kiosk is a very useful way to repurpose an older multimedia computer. An extra monitor can serve as a screen multiplier to allow your booktalks to run in different

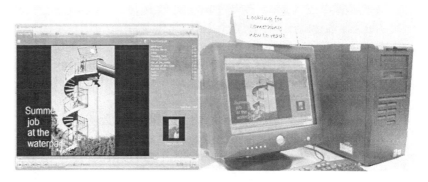

Figure 9.1. A video booktalk kiosk setup using Windows Media Player at a computer station in a school library.

locations. Connect a set of speakers to the kiosk so that people can hear the booktalks. Plan to use low power audio so as not to disturb others. Check that the kiosk computer has the necessary software, such as Media Player for Windows and QuickTime for Macs.

Screen Multiplier

If you want to have your booktalks shown on multiple screens around the library or other location then you will need to use a multiplier. Multipliers are used in computer or video stores to output the same display on multiple screens. A multiplier attached to your computer to display on two screens is an easy way to display the presentation to students as they walk in and while they visit in the library.

Video Splitter to TV

A video splitter sends the presentation to a television from a computer. This system also sends booktalks to a school's closed circuit television system.

You can connect an extra television to the computer as a larger monitor or dual display by sending the video signal from the computer to the television. Some computers already have adapters built in to output a television signal. If yours does not, a Computer-to-TV Video Converter add-on device can be purchased for about $50 from a computer store or an online resource such as Amazon.com. This setup will send the signal out on a school's closed circuit television, also. Then the video booktalks will display in all rooms of the school, such as before the start of the daily announcements.

KIOSK SETUP

To set up your video booktalk kiosk, you will need a computer with the video player software, such as Windows Media Player or QuickTime, and video versions of booktalks or booktalks produced with presentation software, such as PowerPoint. There are sites available on the Internet that share video booktalks (see Chapter 10's Video Booktalking Sites). These sites have video booktalks that were created by students, teachers, school media specialist, and librarians and can be downloaded or played online. Video booktalk sites range in presentation style. Some of the sites provide only a headshot video of a person doing a booktalk, such as the Prairie Middle Students' Video Booktalks, which has QuickTime videos of sixth graders reading their booktalks to a camera. Other sites offer full video of acted presentations, which use sets, actors, and special effects in the booktalks. To start using video booktalks at your school, you can make use of these online video booktalks by adding links to the sites on a class or school Web page.

For your kiosk to remain interesting, you will need an archive of several video booktalks, although you can get started with just a few. To get started, invite the teachers and school media personnel to create a few of their own video booktalks to share or to act as examples for students to use in creating their video booktalks as class projects. These educator- and student-created video booktalks can be stored in your video kiosk and played for everyone to enjoy.

Once the video booktalks have been created or located, they should be saved on the computer and also on a portable medium, such as a CD-ROM or flash drive, for transfer to the computer that will act as the kiosk.

The booktalk kiosk should have the necessary player software installed, such as Windows Media Player or QuickTime, and should be checked for suitability to run the booktalks because installation of additional updates or codecs may be needed. When using the Windows Media Player as the software for the video booktalk kiosk, either use the file menu to open a number of videos, or drag the videos from a folder into the **Now Playing List.** Once you have the collection of videos ready to play, use the **Play** menu to set the player to **Shuffle** (ctrl + h) and **Repeat** (ctrl + t). Your videos will randomly play and will constantly repeat until the stop button is pressed. To set up QuickTime to use a single window to play a collection of videos, repeating and shuffling them, an additional program will be needed to create a playlist. Two example programs that can do this in QuickTime are Movie Jukebox (http://www.mindjar.com/download.html) and QT XList (http://macupdate.com/info.php/id/11981). These are both freeware programs that can create looping playlists that can be used as part of the video kiosk.

POWERPOINT KIOSKS

Begin by creating a booktalk PowerPoint (see Chapter 5 for instructions). You will want to add **Slide Transitions** to ensure your presentation will be visually appealing. Slide transitions are special effects you can use to move from one slide to another in a slide show.

Open an Existing PowerPoint Slide Show

1. In **Slide Sorter View** ensure the **Slide Sorter** toolbar is showing. If not, select it from **Toolbars** in the **View** menu.
2. Click the slide to which you want to apply a transition effect.

   • To apply a transition to a group of slides, click the first slide and hold down the Shift key, then click on the last slide. The group of slides is then selected.

3. After selecting the slide(s) to which you want to add transitions, click the slide transition tool or click the **Slide Show Menu** and choose **Slide Transition.** The **Slide Transition** dialog box appears.
4. Choose the transition effect you want from the drop-down list. View a preview of the transition in the **Effects** window.
5. Choose Slow, Medium, or Fast to control the speed of the transition.
6. Select **Automatically After** and enter the length of time for the slide to appear on the screen before moving to the next slide.
7. Choose to play a sound when the slide is shown. Choose the sound you want from the drop-down list. You can decide to play the sound once or over and over again (loop). If you choose loop, and want the sound to stop when the next slide appears, add the sound called **Stop Previous Sound** to the next slide.
8. Click **Apply.**

Figure 9.2. Computer setup in the school library automatically running PowerPoint booktalks.

Automating Your Presentation

The next thing to do when building a kiosk presentation is to automate the presentation. Do this by setting timings for the slide show.

1. Click the **Slide Show** menu and then click **Rehearse Timings.**
2. Rehearse your slide show in the speed you would like to see it displayed.

   - To advance the rehearsal slide show click the arrow on the rehearsal dialog box.
   - If you have animated texts or images in your slides, you will be able to time the animation as well as the slide transition.

3. When your presentation is finished, a message box appears asking you if you want to record the timings. Click **Yes.** PowerPoint will record the time you spent on each slide and apply the timing to your presentation. Your slide show will now run automatically.
4. Preview the slide show in **Slide Show View.**

PowerPoint in the Kiosk

With PowerPoint, the computer can automatically play the slide show without intervention. This feature will cause your booktalk kiosk to run by itself and attract students to the display.

To create the kiosk:

1. Automate your presentation using the four steps shown previously.
2. Click the **Slide Show** menu then click **Set Up Show.** The **Set Up Show** dialog box appears.
3. Under Show type, click Browsed at a kiosk (full screen).
4. Under Advance slides, click Using timings, if present.
5. Click **OK.** Your presentation is self-running. Once it starts, it will loop over and over until someone presses the Esc key (see Figure 9.2).
6. Preview the slide show in **Slide Show View.**

10

Online Resources for Booktalks

Technology-enhanced booktalks don't necessarily begin with creating them; instead you can start by using existing booktalks. Several online resources provide excellent booktalks that can be presented to your students or can serve as examples of what they can create.

Book Talk! [Tandem Library Books]: http://www.randomhouse.com/teachers/ librarians/booktalks.html

Provides short, written descriptions about the book, the author, ratings, and associated readings.

Booktalk! Module: http://www.bcps.org/offices/lis/models/bktalk

This site from Baltimore County Public Schools is similar to a webquest in presenting how to do a classroom booktalk.

BookTalk.org: http://pub141.ezboard.com/bbooktalk

An online book discussion community and reading group dedicated to reading and discussing quality nonfiction books. While geared to adults, some of the titles may be of interest to teens.

Booktalker: http://www.thebooktalker.com/BTmonthly.htm

Dr. Joni Richards Bodart shares written booktalks on her site.

Booktalking Ideas from the Century 21 Librarian: http://www.albany.edu/ %7edj2930/yabooktalking.html

This site provides multiple ideas on approaches with samples to creating book talks.

Librarians@Random: http://www.randomhouse.com/teachers/librarians/book talks.html

Provides short blurbs about books with cover images—updated with new books each month.

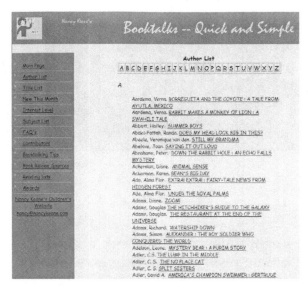

Figure 10.1. Nancy Keane's Booktalks Quick and Simple Web site (http://www.nancykeane.com/booktalks).

Nancy Keane's Booktalks Quick and Simple: http://www.nancykeane.com/booktalks

A booktalking database of over 7,000 ready-to-use booktalks (see Figure 10.1).

Promoting Reading with Book Talks: http://www.det.wa.edu.au/education/cip/learntech/eng/pr

This Department of Education and Training from the Government of Western Australia provides resources, ideas, and training about booktalks.

Teachers@Random: http://www.randomhouse.com/teachers/librarians/booktalks.html

Provides over 500 booktalks.

TeensPoint.org: http://www.teenspoint.org/reading_matters/booktalks.asp

Librarians from the Central Rappahonnock Regional Library share their favorite young adult books though booktalks.

YALSA Booktalking: http://www.ala.org/ala/yalsa/profdev/booktalking.cfm

Provides resources with information and ideas on booktalking for young adults.

Video Booktalk Locations

Apple Education Language Arts: http://education.apple.com/education/ilife/subject_template.php?subject_id=2

Look through the page for "Short Story Commercials" and "Book Ads." Both provide example videos with associated lesson plans.

Book Movie Trailers: http://www.lib.ci.tucson.az.us/trp/trailers.htm

Five video booktalk videos created by teens at the Tucson Pima Public Library.

Booktalk Slideshows: http://www.umiacs.umd.edu/~jimmylin/LBSC690-Final-Project-Gallery/200509-booktalks/booktalks.html#

Three video versions of booktalks presented though still images.

Bookwink: http://www.bookwink.com

Provides 25 video booktalks in sets of 2 or 3 divided by reading topic.

Cougar Paw'dCast: http://professor-marvel.com/podcast/labels/booktalk.html

A number of video booktalks presented by Dalton Middle School students.

Digital Booktalks©: http://www.digital
booktalk.com

Over 40 very high quality production booktalks (QuickTime).

Google Video: http://video.google.com/
videosearch?q=+booktalk&hl=en

A general search of the site found over 200
video booktalks (see Figure 10.2).

HarperCollinsCanada's Trailers for Books:
http://www.harpercollins.ca/trailers

Figure 10.2. Google Video search for booktalks.
Copyright © Google 2007.

Site provides over 15 different books including *Planet Earth* by Tony Juniper, *Run* by
Ann Patchett, and *The Bad Beginning* and *The Reptile Room* by Lemony Snicket.

Picture Book Video Award: http://www.thebookstandard.com/bookstandard/
events/picture_book_video/index.jsp

This single booktalk on the book *Flotsam* won the 2006 picture book video award.

Pima County Public Library Teen Zone: http://www.tppl.org/teenzone/trailers

This site has Teen Trailers (Book Movie Trailers), well-created video booktalks including *Cut, The Stranger, Stones in Water, The House of the Scorpion,* and *Hangman's Curse.*

Prairie Middle Students Video Book Talks: http://www.prairiepride.org/teach
ertools/ViewAssignment.php?AssignID=19589&SylID=327

Seventeen booktalks by middle school students about their selected books.

TeacherTube.com: http://www.teachertube.com/search_result.php?search_id=
booktalk

A large number of video booktalks can be found by simple searching including
Sirena, and *The Tail of Emily Windsnap, Theodosia and the Serpents of Chaos, The Wright 3,*
and *From the Mixed-Up Files of Mrs. Basil E. Frankweiler.*

Teen BookVideo Awards: http://www.thebookstandard.com/bookstandard/
events/teen_book_video/index.jsp

Shows the top three book videos for teen books.

VidLit: http://vidlit.com

Provides over 60 booktalk videos.

YouTube.com: http://www.youtube.com/results?search_query=booktalk

A large number of video booktalks can be found by simple searching including *Fly on
the Wall, Born to Rock, Warriors into the Wild, The King of Attolia, Midnight Bayou, The Giver,
The Rules of Survival, Helen Keller, The Yiddish Policeman's Union,* and *Fanboy and Gothgirl.*

11

Assessment

A number of evaluation tools and instruments are available for educators to assess student performance in their technology-enhanced booktalks. One of the best such instruments of evaluation is the rubric. Rubrics are used to evaluate the quality of student work on a complex project, using indicators in several categories. Specific descriptions of performance of a given task at several different levels of quality are created. Students and teachers use rubrics to evaluate performance on the tasks, both formative and summative. Students are often given the rubric in advance to assist with self-evaluation, and in some cases they may even help develop it, so they know in advance the expectations of them.

Teachers should check resources, such as Rubistar (see Figure 11.1), where evaluation tools have been posted by teachers, along with guidelines for creating evaluation resources. Look under topics other than booktalks, including topics such as Multimedia Projects and Digital Storytelling. Search tools such as Google will also help you find other teachers' booktalk rubrics, which can be adapted.

RUBRIC TOOLS

Assessment Generators: http://www.thecanadianteacher.com/tools/assessment

Building a Rubric@2Learn.ca: http://www.2learn.ca/construct/rubric/tlcrubric.html

Project based learning: http://4teachers.org/projectbased

Roobrix: http://roobrix.com

Figure 11.1. Rubistar is an online rubric creation tool. RubiStar © 2000–2008 ALTEC at the University of Kansas. Development of this educational resource was supported, in part, by the U.S. Department of Education award #R302A000015 to ALTEC (Advanced Learning Technologies in Education Consortia) at the University of Kansas.

Rubric Builder: http://landmark-project.com/classweb/tools/rubric_builder.php
Rubric Processor: http://rubricprocessor.com
Rubrics Generator: http://www.teach-nology.com/web_tools/rubrics
Rubrics/Rubric Makers: http://www.teach-nology.com/web_tools/rubrics
Rubristar: http://rubistar.4teachers.org

	4	3	2	1
Setting	Lots of vivid, descriptive words are used to tell the audience when and where the story takes place.	Some vivid, descriptive words are used to tell the audience when and where the story takes place.	The audience can figure out when and where the story took place, but there isn't much detail (e.g., once upon a time in a land far, far away).	The audience has trouble telling when and where the story takes place.
Characters	The main characters are named and clearly described (through words and/or actions). The audience knows and can describe what the characters look like and how they typically behave.	The main characters are named and described (through words and/or actions). The audience has a fairly good idea of what the characters look like.	The main characters are named. The audience knows very little about the main characters.	It is hard to tell who the main characters are.
Problem	It is very easy for the audience to understand what problem the main character(s) face and why it is a problem.	It is fairly easy for the audience to understand what problem the main character(s) face and why it is a problem.	It is fairly easy for the audience to understand what problem the main character(s) face, but it is not clear why it is a problem.	It is not clear what problem the main character(s) face.
Knows the Story	The booktalker knows the story well and has obviously practiced the booktalk several times. There is no need for notes, and the speaker speaks with confidence.	The booktalker knows the story pretty well and has practiced the booktalk once or twice. May need notes once or twice, but the speaker is relatively confident.	The booktalker knows some of the story, but did not appear to have practiced. May need notes 3–4 times, and the speaker appears ill-at-ease.	The booktalker could not tell the story without using notes.

Self/Peer Evaluation

Name:_____ Digital Story Title:_____

Date: _____

Entry #1: *Give yourself and your group members a grade on this project. Describe each person's contribution to the project.*

My grade: A A – B + B B – C + C C – D + D D – F

My contribution to the project:

Group member's name:

Group member's grade: A A – B + B B – C + C C – D + D D – F

Group member's contribution to the project:

Everyone Has a Story to Tell...and We'll Help You Tell It

Digital Storytelling Rubric
Names:
Digital Story Title:

	Excellent	Good	Satisfactory	Needs Improvement
Title ____/5	The title is creative and is easy to read. The title sets the mood for the story. (5 points)	The title could be more creative but sets the mood for the story. (3–4 points)	The title is creative but does not help set the mood of the story. (2 points)	The title does not relate to the mood of the story and could be more creative. (0–1 point)
Point of View—Purpose ____/10	Establishes a purpose early and maintains a clear focus throughout the story. (10 points)	Establishes a purpose early and maintains the focus throughout most of the story. (8–9 points)	There are a few times where focus is not clear. (5–7 points)	It is difficult to figure out the purpose of the story. (0–4 points)
Mood of the Story ____/15	The mood of your story is evident to the audience and is supported with all of your images, audio, and titles. (15 points)	The mood of your story is evident to the audience and is supported with some of your images, audio, and titles. (11–14 points)	The mood of your story is not always clear to the audience and is supported with some of your images, audio, and titles. (5–10 points)	The mood of your story is not clear to the audience, and the images, audio, and titles do not support the mood. (0–4 points)
Accuracy of Facts (Content) ____/15	All supportive facts are reported accurately. The quotes and facts and other information is relevant to the story and present the theme of the story. (15 points)	Almost all supportive facts are reported accurately. The information is relevant to the story, but some does not relate to the theme of the story. (11–14 points)	Most supportive facts are reported accurately. Some of the information is not relevant and does not help illustrate the theme of the story. (5–10 points)	NO facts are reported OR most are inaccurately reported. The information is not relevant and does not add to the theme of the story. (0–4 points)

	Excellent	Good	Satisfactory	Needs Improvement
Sequencing ____/10	Details are placed in a logical order. The combination of video, audio, graphics, and titles is presented in an effective way to present the theme and support the mood. (10 points)	Details are placed in a logical order through most of the story. The combination of video, audio, graphics, and titles is presented in an effective way to present the theme and support the mood. (8–9 points)	Details are not placed in a logical order. The combination of video, audio, graphics, and titles is not presented in an effective way to present the theme and support the mood. (5–7 points)	Details are not placed in a logical order. The combination of the video, audio, graphics, and titles does not support the theme or convey the mood of the story. (0–4 points)
Time ____/5	The story is told with exactly the right amount of detail throughout. It does not seem too short or too long. (5 points)	The story is good, though it seems to drag somewhat OR needs slightly more detail in one or two sections. (4 points)	The story seems to need more editing. It is noticeably too long or too short in more than one section. (2–3 points)	The story needs extensive editing. It is too long or too short to be interesting. (0–1 points)
Script ____/15	Script is complete with a description of what is on the screen. Script reflects outstanding planning and organization for the visuals and audio for the story. All sources are written on the script. (15 points)	Script has some description of what is on the screen. Script reflects some planning and organization for the visuals and audio for the story. All sources are written on the script. (11–14 points)	Script has very little descriptions of what is on the screen. Script reflects very little planning and organization for the visuals and audio for the story. Some sources are not included on the script. (5–10 points)	Script is incomplete. There is little evidence of planning for the story. Sources are missing from the script. (0–4 points)

	Excellent	Good	Satisfactory	Needs Improvement
Appearance _____/15	The clips are edited effectively to create emotion and mood. All of the selections relate to the topic and are clear and easy to understand. The images and titles appear for the appropriate length of time. Titles are used to identify the people interviewed. Transitions and effects are used appropriately and effectively. (15 points)	The clips are edited and related to the topic. They are clear, but not easy to understand. The images and titles appear for the appropriate length of time. Titles are used to identify people interviewed. Most of the transitions and effects are used appropriately. (11–14 points)	The clips are not all related to the topic and add to the mood. Most of the selections relate to the topic. The images and titles do not appear for the appropriate length. Titles are used to identify people interviewed. The transitions and effects are not used effectively. (5–10 points)	The clips are not all related to the topic and add to the mood. Most of the selections do not relate to the topic. The images and titles do not appear for the appropriate length. There are no transitions or effects used effectively. Titles are not used to identify people interviewed. (0–4 points)
Sources & Credits _____/10	All sources used for quotes and facts are credible and cited correctly. The sources are accurately cited in the credits. (10 points)	All sources used for quotes and facts are credible and, most are cited correctly. The sources are accurately cited in the credits. (8–9 points)	Most sources used for quotes and facts are credible and cited correctly. The sources are included in the credits but not accurately cited. (5–7 points)	Many sources used for quotes and facts are less than credible (suspect) and/or are not cited correctly. There are missing sources from the credits, and they are inaccurately cited. (0–4 points)

TOTAL:
_____/ 100

Additional Comments:

Adapted from S. Behmer's Digital Storytelling Rubric http://projects.educ.iastate.edu/~ds/Behmer/Rubric.htm

From *Tech-Savvy Booktalkers: A Guide for 21st-Century Educators* by Nancy J. Keane and Terence W. Cavanaugh. Westport, CT: Libraries Unlimited. Copyright © 2009.

Digital Story Checklist

Names:_____

Digital Story Title:_____

Your digital story should include the following things:

A clear theme and mood

A catchy title (may include a subtitle) that draws the interest of the audience

Audio with appropriate timing and volume

Audio that adds to the mood of your story

Visuals with appropriate timing

Visuals (titles, pictures, video) that add to the mood of your story

Transitions that add to the mood of your story

Accurate statistics and information from your research

All audio, video, and graphics are cited correctly for your credits

Include a thank you to those who were interviewed for your story

Credits that are easy to read and include all sources, authors' first names, and the date it was produced

Script Requirements

All audio, pictures, and video sources are cited on your script

A description of what will be on the screen from your outline

Narration by the authors written

Script must be approved by the teacher before you begin work on the computer

Adapted from *S. Behmer's Digital Story Checklist* (http://projects.educ.iastate.edu/ ~ds/Behmer/Checklist.htm)

Adapted from *Rubrics for Digital Storytelling Class by Meg Ormiston* (meg@ techteachers.com) at http://www.techteachers.com/digstory/gradclass/rubrics.htm

Rubric for Storyboard

CATEGORY	1	2	3	4
Content	The story is not aligned to the Learning Standards.	There is evidence of standards, but they do not align with the project.	Some of the standards are addressed.	The story is aligned to the Learning Standards.
Process	There is no evidence of a storyline.	The story is difficult to follow.	The story is complete, yet lacking depth.	The story is easy to follow and shows significant planning.
Format and Technology Use	The story is incomplete.	The story needs editing.	The story needs additional editing.	The technology supports the story.

Rubric for Final Digital Story

CATEGORY	1	2	3	4
Content	The story is not complete.	The digital story is missing significant elements.	The digital story is completed, yet the content is not grade level appropriate.	The digital story is grade level appropriate and engaging for students.
Quality of Proposed Projects	The digital story meets the minimum requirements.	The digital story needs more details added.	The digital story is engaging, visually attractive, yet it is not complete for classroom use.	The digital story is engaging, visually attractive, and ready to be used in the classroom.
Format and Technology Use	The project does not have a storyboard.	The project is emerging, but needs supporting details	Project is completed, yet more editing is needed.	Project is nicely presented including sound and visual images.
Aligns to State Learning Standards	No standards are listed.	The standards are listed but do not align with the project.	Standards are clearly identified.	The standards are clearly identified and appropriate to the unit of instruction.

Rubric for Soundtrack

CATEGORY	1	2	3	4
Content	There is no soundtrack.	The soundtrack takes away from the presentation.	The soundtrack needs some editing.	The soundtrack supports the digital story.
Quality of Proposed Projects	The soundtrack does not match the story.	The soundtrack distracts from the story.	The music needs editing to support the story.	The soundtrack matches the mood and pace of the story.
Format and Technology Use	The student cannot work with the soundtrack.	The soundtrack does not match the story.	The soundtrack needs editing.	The participant can independently create a soundtrack.

Rubric for Reflection Activities

CATEGORY	1	2	3	4
Content	The assignment does not align to the topic.	The assignment aligns to the topic, yet it does not include personal reflection.	The assignment clearly demonstrates reflection on the topic.	The assignment clearly demonstrates opinions and reflection on the topic.
Quality of Proposed Projects	Includes only a few sentences.	Includes one to three paragraphs with errors.	Includes one to three well-written paragraphs with few errors.	Includes one to three well-written paragraphs with no errors.
Format and Technology Use	The assignment does not include the use of technology.	The assignment was submitted to the instructor on time on paper.	The assignment was submitted to the instructor on time on paper.	The assignment was submitted to the instructor on time and digitally.

Appendix A

Millennial Generation Students

Once, schools taught the baby boomers, and then came generations X and Y. Today's students are often known as the *millennials* or the *millennial generation.* What makes this generation different is that they are the first generation of people who were born into, have grown up with, and come of age with the Internet and computer technology. This population of nearly 50 million students in our schools represents the largest and most diverse group in our educational history.

Susan Patrick, when serving as Director of Educational Technology for the U.S. Department of Education, described the technological world of the millennials as being quite different from previous educational generations (see Figure A.1). For example, with the previous generation, the number of hours that students spent watching television was a concern, but with the millennials, time spent by teens watching television has been surpassed by use of the Internet. The following are just some of the characteristics of these new information age students (Patrick, 2004).

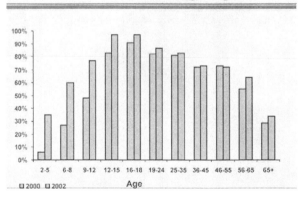

Figure A.1. Internet use by age.
Source: UCLA Center for Communications Policy (2003, February). UCLA Internet Report: Surveying the Digital Future, Year Three. Retrieved July 27, 2007 from http://www.digital.org/pdf/InternetReportYear Three.pdf.

Corporation for Public Broadcasting. (2002). *Connected to the Future: A Report on Children's Internet Use;* Retrieved July 28, 2007 from http://www.cpb.org/ Stations/reports/connected/connected_report.pdf.

Pew Report (2003, April). The Ever-Shifting Internet Population. Pew Internet & American Life Project. Retrieved July 26, 2007 from http://www.pewinternet. org/PPF/r/15presentation_display.asp.

MILLENNIAL SECONDARY STUDENTS

- 28% of high school students access foreign news sources via the Internet.
- 94% of online teens use the Internet for school-related research.
- 71% of online teens indicate they rely on Internet sources for projects.
- 48% of teens think that the Internet improves their relationships.

- 74% of online teens use instant messaging.
- 24% of online teens have created their own Web pages or sites.

MILLENNIAL ELEMENTARY STUDENTS

- 72% of first graders used a home computer during the summer on a weekly basis.
- Over 85% of young children with home computers use them for educational purposes.
- 97% of kindergartners in 1999 had access to a computer at school or home.
- 35% of 2–5 year old children use the Internet.
- 13% of children ages 7 and under own a wireless device.

Appendix B

Do's and Don't's
of Booktalking

There are definitely some rules of thumb involving booktalking. However, remember that nothing is written in stone. Your booktalks should reflect your own style and personality and the needs of your audience.

DO

Bring the books with you. Enthusiasm increases if the children can see the physical book. If it is not possible, you can substitute a color copy of the cover or a color overhead transparency so that the children can at least see the cover.

Have realistic expectations. Some booktalks will create more enthusiasm than others. Sometimes children just aren't in the mood to listen.

Learn the booktalks. This gives a spontaneous, connected feel to the presentation. If you cannot memorize the booktalks, have a cheat sheet with you that you can hide behind the book, and refer to it only as needed.

Be prepared to ad lib. Don't be afraid to vary from the script. You may find that you can relate a talk to a particular group in a way that you didn't anticipate.

When booktalking multiple titles, vary themes. If you are talking about a specific theme, vary the type of book—one humorous, one serious—one upbeat, one dark.

Vary the length of the booktalks. It breaks up the presentation and is much more interesting. You might want to include short, one-line descriptions of books in between the booktalks.

Be organized, cool, and confident. Show that you know the books and want the children to read them, too.

Relax and enjoy. Have fun with it.

Start strong and end strong. Try to choose a really dynamic booktalk to end your presentation. Leave them wanting more.

Keep records of books used. This is particularly important if you booktalk to the same group more than once. You don't want to keep repeating yourself.

Learn from your mistakes. If you have a booktalk that bombs, rethink it and rewrite it.

DON'T

Booktalk books you haven't read. It will show. You may lose your credibility with the audience.

Booktalk books you didn't like. Again, people will pick up on it. If they don't and they choose the book based on your booktalk, your credibility will be questioned if the children don't like the book either.

Gush or oversell. You'll sound phony. You also risk setting up false expectations in the minds of the listeners.

Give away the ending or surprise. Never tell the ending. Why would anyone want to bother to read the book if they know how it ends?

Give a book review. That is a different presentation altogether. You are just advertising the books. You are not giving report on the literary merit of the title.

Label by gender/race/other. Books should not be referred to as "boy books" or other labels. Each book can be enjoyed by anyone.

Read long passages from the book unless you have to. You may want to give the flavor of the writing style, but usually it's more effective if you try to stay away from reading.

Talk about sex/drugs/violence without clearing it with the teacher/parents. There are times to bring up controversial topics in schools, but be sure that this is the time.

Booktalk books you don't own. It is very frustrating for children to hear about a book only to find that they don't have access to it.

Be boring to yourself. If you are boring yourself, imagine how the audience feels.

Start booktalks with booktalks. Always introduce the topic/theme and tell the children a little about what they can expect to hear in the next few minutes.

Appendix C

File Extensions

The following are common file extensions that you may come across when using or creating booktalks with technology.

.aa—Audible audio book format
.aif/.aifc/.aiff—audio
.asf—audio/video
.au—digital audio format
.aup—Audacity project file
.avi—Windows video format
.band—Garage Band project file
.bmp—bitmap, uncompressed image file
.dib—image
.doc—Microsoft Word document file
.docx—Microsoft Word 2007 document file
.emf—image
.exe—an executable program file
.flv—FLASH video format
.fss—Flash Slideshow Maker Project file
.gif—image format designed for drawings
.htm/.html—hypertext markup language for web browsers
.jpg/JPEG: image format designed for photographs
.knt—KeyNote presentation file
.mov—QuickTime video
.mpa—audio
.mp3—digital audio format
.mp4—enhanced podcast file
.mpg—MPEG—video format
.mswmm—Windows Movie Maker project file
.odt—Open Office word processing document
.pct—Mac bitmap image file
.pdf—Adobe Reader file
.png/PING: image format for photographs or drawings
.pps—PowerPoint show file
.ppt—PowerPoint presentation file

.pptx—PowerPoint 2007 presentation file

.ra—real media video

.rss—special text file used for podcast/blog subscriptions

.rtf—rich text format

.seb—Franklin eBookman Format

.snd—audio

.swf—Macromedia FLASH format

.sxi—Open Office Impress File

.tif/TIFF—Tagged image file format for high-resolution graphics

.txt—Plain text format

.wav—uncompressed audio file

.wma—Windows media audio format

.wmf—Windows media image format

.wmv—Window's media video format

.wp3—MS PhotoStory project file

.wpd—WordPerfect document

.xml—Extensible Markup Language, similar to .htm/.html, used for describing data

Appendix D

Booktalks—They're Not Just for Libraries Anymore!

When you think about booktalks, you probably envision a librarian speaking to a group of library users. The librarian may be focusing on a group of books by theme, author, or genre. But there are many other uses for booktalks and many other prospective book-talkers.

COMMUNITY PROJECT/OUTREACH (PARENTS/GUESTS/ETC.)

Booktalks given by librarians, school media specialists, teachers, or students can be presented to community groups as an outreach tool. These can be presented during a parent night or event at the school or library. By adding a technology enhancement to the booktalk, you have now expanded your reach. Save a PowerPoint booktalk for airing on the local public access television station. Videotape your booktalks and post them on your library Web page or upload to YouTube. Be sure to add a link to the booktalk on your Web page. Use audio technology and provide a booktalk podcast. Be sure to add an RSS feed so that the community members can subscribe.

Another way to reach out to the community is to have guest booktalkers. Parents, politicians, business people, and so forth can be asked to record a booktalk for your library. Have a local doctor booktalk a book dealing with making good choices. Have the football coach booktalk a book about high school sports. Have the mayor booktalk a book about elections. You will probably have to supply the booktalk.

STUDENTS

Students are often the target of booktalks, but they are also very good at giving booktalks. For many years, teachers have been assigning traditional booktalks in place of the standard book report. But now we need to take it up a notch and have the students infuse technology into the booktalk.

Student-produced booktalks can be used on the school Web page, on the local public access television or public radio station, or even on the school's morning announcements. They can also be used with younger students. It is not unusual for students to have younger reading buddies. Student-generated booktalks can work very well with reading buddies.

TEACHER INTEGRATION

Teachers are another sector that can use booktalks very effectively. Most teachers have classroom libraries that they can draw on for booktalks. Students are more apt to pick up a book and try it when it is introduced by the teacher.

Literature Circle Introduction

A literature circle is a student-centered reading activity for a group of 4–6 students at any grade level. Each member of a circle is assigned a role that helps guide the group in a discussion of the title they are all reading. Literature circles provide an opportunity for students to control their own learning and to share thoughts, concerns, and their understanding of the events of the novel. The books read during literature circles are most often student selected. Booktalks are the perfect introduction to the books that the students can choose. The booktalk will get the students interested in reading a particular book and will also focus their thoughts on an important aspect that can be emphasized during the booktalk.

Sustained Silent Reading

Sustained silent reading (SSR) is a time set aside during the school day when children can read independently in books of their own selection.

"Research has shown that reading ability is positively correlated with the extent to which students read recreationally," according to the "Reading and Writing Habits of Students" section of *The Condition of Education 1997*, published by the National Center for Education Statistics. "Educators are increasingly encouraging their students to read and write on their own."

Using booktalks to introduce students to a variety of titles is a very effective way to get them reading during SSR time. When students are surrounded by books and introduced to them by their teacher, they are more apt to pick up a book they might have overlooked otherwise.

LIBRARIAN INTEGRATION

Part of the library media specialist's duties is booktalking to students. This can be done in the school library or in the classroom. By infusing technology into this routine, the library media specialist can reach out beyond the library.

Booktalks can be delivered during the morning announcements. These can be done over an audio announcement system. If the school has a video system, booktalks can be delivered via the morning news show.

READING COACH/LITERACY COACH

A reading coach/literacy coach is a teacher whose primary role is providing classroom teachers and other instructional staff members with strategies, tools, and techniques to effectively teach reading to all students. In this role, the coach will be introducing both teachers and students to books. The use of technology-enhanced booktalks provides an effective way to do this.

Index

About the Authors

TERENCE CAVANAUGH teaches teachers about educational technology in Florida. A devoted fan of both technology and reading (especially science fiction), he is always excited when his two passions meet. Terry has been an author for a number of books, including *Literature Circles with Technology* and *The Digital Reader: E-Books in K12 Education.* Terry and his wife, Cathy, maintain the Web site *DrsCavanaugh Educational Technology* (http://www.drscavanaugh.org) with resources for teachers concerning the integration of technology into the educational setting with topics including electronic books, distance learning, digital cameras, and science education. The Web site provides links to over 200 resources for thousands of free electronic forms of books (eBooks) that can be used with students. Terry received his B.S. in science education from the University of Florida, an M.Ed. in Physics Education from the University of Central Florida, and a Ph.D. in Educational Technology from the University of South Florida. Currently, he is an instructor of educational technology at the University of North Florida's College of Education and Human Services. Terry lives in Jacksonville, Florida, with his wife and his science fiction books.

NANCY J. KEANE is a school library media specialist in New Hampshire. She has been a lover of children's literature all her life, so working with books and children is a perfect match for her. In addition to her work in the school, Nancy also hosts a television show on local television. *Kids Book Beat* is a monthly show that features children from the area booktalking their favorite books. Nancy is the author of an award-winning Web site Booktalks—Quick and Simple (http://www.nancykeane.com/booktalks). The site has proven to be indispensable to library media specialists and teachers around the world. The database includes over 7,000 ready-to-use booktalks, and contributions are welcome from educators and students. Additionally, Nancy has a page of thematic booklists available on her page. *Atn Reading Lists* consists of about 1,900 thematic lists culled from suggestions from several professional e-mail discussion lists. Nancy received a B.A. in child psychology from the University of Massachusetts, Amherst, an M.L.S. from University of Rhode Island, and a M.A. in Educational Technology from George Washington University and is currently doing her doctoral work at Rivier College. She is an adjunct faculty member at New Hampshire Technical College, Plymouth State University, and the University of Rhode Island. She also presents workshops and seminars on children's literature. Nancy has won numerous awards for her work. Nancy lives in Concord, New Hampshire, with her children and grandchildren. They share their home with an assortment of animals.

LaVergne, TN USA
22 November 2010
205971LV00002B/10/P